DESCARTES: A GUIDE FOR THE PERPLEXED

Continuum's Guides for the Perplexed are clear, concise and accessible introductions to thinkers, writers and subjects that students and readers can find especially challenging. Concentrating specifically on what it is that makes the subject difficult to grasp, these books explain and explore key themes and ideas, guiding the reader towards a thorough understanding of demanding material.

DESCARTES: A GUIDE FOR THE PERPLEXED

JUSTIN SKIRRY

continuum

Continuum International Publishing Group
The Tower Building   80 Maiden Lane
11 York Road   Suite 704
London SE1 7NX   New York NY10038

www.continuumbooks.com

First published 2008

British Library Cataloguing-in-Publication Data
A catalogue record for this book is available from the British Library.

ISBN-10: HB: 0–8264–8985–0
PB: 0–8264–8986–9

ISBN-13: HB: 978–0–8264–8985–2
PB: 978–0–8264–8986–9

Library of Congress Cataloging-in-Publication Data
Skirry, Justin.
Descartes : a guide for the perplexed / Justin Skirry.
p. cm.
Includes bibliographical references (p.   ) and index.
ISBN 978–0–8264–8985–2 – ISBN 978–0–8264–8986–9
1. Descartes, René, 1596–1650.   I. Title.
B1873.S55 2008
194–dc22
2007027773

Typeset by RefineCatch Limited, Bungay, Suffolk
Printed and bound by MPG Books Ltd, Bodmin, Cornwall

CONTENTS

CONTENTS

ACKNOWLEDGEMENTS

First and foremost I would like to thank the editors at Continuum for their understanding and support in completing this project. I would also like to thank all those at the Cochrane-Woods Library of Nebraska Wesleyan University for their tireless efforts and dedicated service. Finally, I would like to thank my research assistant Kiran Bhardwaj for her fresh eye and insightful comments and criticisms.

ABBREVIATIONS

AT   Descartes, René (1974–89, Charles Adam and
            Paul Tannery, eds), *Œuvre de Descartes*, 11 vols.
            References are made to volume and page number.
CSM/CSMK   Descartes, René (1984–91, John Cottingham,
            Robert Stoothoff, Dugald Murdoch and Anthony
            Kenny, trans.), *The Philosophical Writings of
            Descartes*, 3 vols. References are made to volume and
            page number.

For my wife
Sarah Jane

INTRODUCTION

René Descartes was born to Joachim Descartes and Jeanne Brochard on 31 March 1596 in La Haye, near Tours, France. The Descartes clan was a bourgeois family composed of mostly doctors and some lawyers. Joachim Descartes was a lawyer who spent most of his career as a member of provincial French parliaments. After the death of their mother, which occurred soon after René's birth, the Descartes children (René, his sister Jeanne and brother Pierre) were sent to live with their maternal grandmother, Jeanne Sain. They remained with her until their father remarried in 1600. Not much is known about his early childhood, but René is thought to have been a sickly and fragile child, so much so that when he was sent to board at the Jesuit college at La Flèche at Easter 1607, he was not obligated to rise at 5:00am with the other boys for morning prayers but was allowed to rest until 10:00am Mass. At La Flèche Descartes completed the usual courses of study as well as the philosophical curriculum with courses in the 'verbal arts' of grammar, rhetoric and dialectic (or logic) and the 'mathematical arts' which comprised arithmetic, music, geometry and astronomy. His course of study at the college was capped off with courses in metaphysics, natural philosophy and ethics. Descartes graduated from La Flèche in 1614.

In 1615–16 Descartes received a degree in civil and canon law from the University of Poitiers. However, despite his degree, he never pursued a law career. Instead, he chose to see the world as a volunteer in the army of Maurice of Nassau. It is during this time that he met Isaac Beekman, who was perhaps the most important influence on his early adulthood. It was Beekman who rekindled Descartes' interest in science and opened his eyes to the possibility of applying mathematical techniques to other fields. Descartes, however, remained a soldier and was stationed at Ulm in Germany where he had three dreams that gave him a vision of a universal science and inspired a search for a new method. Descartes began his work on a method entitled *Rules for the Direction of the Mind* at about this time, sporadically working on it from about 1620 until finally abandoning the project for good in 1628.

It was also in 1628 that Descartes moved to the Netherlands. He remained there, despite frequent changes of address, until he moved to Sweden at the invitation of Queen Christina in late 1649. He moved to the Netherlands to achieve a solitude and quiet that he could not attain with all the distractions of Paris. It was here in 1629 that Descartes began work on *The World*, which was intended to provide a mechanistic picture of the world. But the condemnation of Galileo led him to suppress its publication (see Chapter 6.1 for more). Although many of its principles and explanations were published in later works, *The World* itself never saw the light of day. However, this did not deter him from his own scientific enquiries or from providing mechanistic explanations for a wide variety of phenomena. Some of these findings were published in French in 1637 in the form of three essays entitled *Geometry*, *Dioptics* and *Meteors*, which had a preface attached to them entitled *Discourse on Method*. The fact that they were published not in Latin but in the vernacular indicates that these essays and the *Discourse* were intended for a more popular audience. On a personal note, Descartes' daughter, Francine, was born during the research for these essays in 1635. Her mother was a maid at the home where Descartes was staying. Unfortunately, Francine died of a fever in 1640 at the age of five while Descartes was making arrangements for her education in France.

Descartes began work in 1639 on his seminal philosophical text, *Meditations on First Philosophy*. Before its publication, Descartes solicited objections from some of the most learned men of his day. The first edition of the *Meditations* was published in Latin in 1641 with six sets of objections and his replies. A second edition published in 1642 also included a seventh set of objections and replies as well as a letter to Fr Dinet in which he defended his philosophy against charges of religious unorthodoxy. Descartes went on to publish his philosophy, including much of his physics, in a textbook called *Principles of Philosophy* in a Latin edition in 1644. Both the *Meditations* and *Principles* were republished in French in 1647 for a wider, more popular audience.

Princess Elizabeth of Bohemia, who had read the *Meditations*, struck up a long and fruitful correspondence with Descartes in 1643. Although her letters begin with questions about how an immaterial mind can cause voluntary motion in the body, it becomes quickly apparent that her concerns are moral in nature. This discussion of morals and the nature of the passions or emotions eventually culminated in Descartes' last published work, *Passions of the Soul*. During this time, another royal, Queen Christina of Sweden, also initiated a correspondence with Descartes wherein morals and the absolute good were discussed. This eventually led to an invitation for Descartes to join her court in Stockholm. Although Descartes had reservations about going, he eventually accepted Christina's invitation. In September 1649 Descartes arrived in Sweden where he was asked to rise at 5:00am to meet the Queen to discuss philosophy, contrary to his usual habit, developed at La Flèche, of sleeping in late. His decision to go to Sweden, however, was ill-fated: Descartes died of pneumonia on 11 February 1650.

THE MODERN TURN

Descartes is one of many early-seventeenth-century thinkers to make a radical break with the traditional Aristotelian philosophy and science that had dominated the schools of Europe for centuries. Descartes departed from this deeply entrenched, scholastic tradition in at least two important ways. First, Aristotle and his followers believed that all knowledge must come from sensation such that one must see, hear, touch, taste and/or smell something before one can understand it. Descartes broke with this tradition by arguing that immaterial things, i.e. things not perceivable by sensation, such as the soul and God, are better known than material or sensible things. He also broke with this aspect of the traditional doctrine by endorsing the existence of innate ideas, which are not derived from sensation but are implanted in the mind by God. This means that philosophy can be done without recourse to the senses and the uncertainty that accompanies them, whereas innate ideas, which have God as their author, are absolutely certain and free from doubt (see Chapters 2 and 5).

Descartes' second major point of departure concerns models of scientific explanation. Aristotle and his scholastic followers tried to explain physical phenomena through the powers that those things possess. For instance, a scholastic-Aristotelian explanation for why opium puts people to sleep would be that having the power to put people to sleep is part of the nature of opium. Although this is true, it is not very informative: it does not really explain how that power works. Descartes, and other moderns, believed that this ability to put people to sleep could be best explained through an examination of the size, shape and motion of the opium's microscopic parts. In this way, the explanatory order is reversed in that the power to put people to sleep does not explain why opium can do this, but rather the mechanical explanation of how opium can do this explains the existence of the power itself. Accordingly, Descartes endorses a radical change in world-view from a world manifesting a system of unexplained, mysterious powers to viewing the world as a machine wherein intelligible explanations of physical phenomena can be found (for more see Chapters 1 and 6).

THE TREE OF PHILOSOPHY

In the preface to the French edition of his textbook, *Principles of Philosophy*, Descartes uses a tree as a metaphor for his holistic view of philosophy:

> The roots are metaphysics, the trunk is physics, and the branches emerging from the trunk are all the other sciences, which may be reduced to three principal ones, namely medicine, mechanics and morals. (AT IXB 14: CSM I 186)

Although he does not elaborate on this image, it is a helpful way of understanding Descartes' philosophical project. The main thrust is that all the other sciences are ultimately based on the secure roots of metaphysics. This is a very difficult task, which takes most of the *Meditations* to accomplish. In the present work, Chapter 2 establishes the cornerstone of his metaphysics, namely his own existence as well as the nature of the 'I' or self that exists. This seed then grows into the metaphysical roots of this tree as discussed in Chapter 3. This, in turn, provides the basis for his arguments for God's existence in Chapter 4, which also addresses other aspects of his religious thought. Finally, the roots take firm hold in Chapter 5 where it is discovered that only knowledge of God's existence and the fact that he cannot be a deceiver can form an absolutely certain foundation for knowledge upon which the certainty of all the other sciences can be based. With this metaphysical foundation for knowledge in place, the trunk of the tree is now able to grow as examined in Chapter 6's discussion of Descartes' physics. Chapter 7 examines his theory of human nature, which is at least partially based on his physics and is the starting point for any discussion of mechanics, medicine and morals. Although Descartes never developed a full theory of medicine, the sections on the mechanisms of the human body or physiology and the passions found in Chapter 8 point in this direction. Finally, the branch of morals is examined at the end of that chapter. But before delving into any of this, an understanding of the method by which Descartes reaches his conclusions is in order.

On a final note: all English translations are those provided in the volumes translated by John Cottingham *et al.* unless otherwise noted. The reader should also be aware that citations made directly to the *Principles of Philosophy* and the *Passions of the Soul* are to Part and section. For example, *Principles* I.25 refers to Part 1, section 25 of this work.

Justin Skirry
Nebraska Wesleyan University
Lincoln, NE
6 July 2007

CHAPTER I

METHOD

Understanding how a philosopher reaches his conclusions is very important for understanding all facets of his work. This chapter examines Descartes' method in order to see how his philosophical tree is planted and how it grows. The chapter begins with a look at traditional forms of argument and scientific enquiry and Descartes' criticisms of them. The next six sections examine the geometrical nature of his new method in some detail. The chapter then culminates in a discussion of his famous method of doubt and how it facilitates the geometric method in metaphysics.

1.1 CRITICISM OF THE SYLLOGISM

As mentioned in the Introduction, Descartes criticized much of the scholastic-Aristotelian tradition as it was taught in the schools of his day. Their system of logic based on Aristotle's *Prior* and *Posterior Analytics* known as 'dialectic' was no exception. Dialectics dealt with argument forms known as 'syllogisms', which are arguments composed of two premises and a conclusion. Aristotelian dialectics was made up of a set of syllogistic argument forms that preserved truth from premises to conclusion such that if the truth of the premises is known, then the conclusion's truth is also known. The rules were complex and the argument forms relatively few, and so one argument could be composed of several, inter-locking syllogisms. Accordingly, deciphering and criticizing these arguments was complicated and required significant training and expertise.

At the heart of Descartes' distaste for dialectic is his belief that this system of logic does not help, but hinders the use of people's natural reasoning abilities by 'dimming' their naturally clear light of reason:

As for other mental operations which dialectic claims to direct with the help of those already mentioned, they are of no use here, or rather should be reckoned a positive hindrance, for nothing can be added to the clear light of reason which does not in some way dim it. (AT X 372–373: CSM I 16)

Dialectic is also a hindrance, because it makes people intellectually lazy:

[The dialecticians] prescribe certain forms of reasoning in which the conclusions follow with such irresistible necessity that if our reason relies on them, even though it takes, as it were, a rest from considering a particular inference clearly and attentively, it can nevertheless draw a conclusion which is certain simply in virtue of the form. (AT X 405–6: CSM I 36)

Here Descartes makes the observation that people can become so overly reliant on dialectic that they merely follow the rules without the clear and attentive mental focus necessary for apprehending the connections comprising a given inference.

These criticisms declare people's independence from the fetters of scholastic logic by affirming their natural ability to reason and discover the truth, for 'the power of judging well and of distinguishing the true from the false . . . is naturally equal in all men' (AT VI 2: CSM I 111). Accordingly, anyone can discover the truth on her own, as Eudoxus points out to Polyander (literally 'Everyman') in *The Search for Truth*:

All these points have been stated and worked out not by means of logic, or a rule or pattern of argument, but simply by the light of reason and good sense. When this light operates on its own, it is less liable to go wrong than when it anxiously strives to follow the numerous different rules, the inventions of human ingenuity and idleness, which serve more to corrupt it than render it more perfect. (AT X 521: CSM II 415)

These passages indicate that people's natural reasoning abilities are sufficient for discovering the truth, while reliance on dialectic hinders this ability by either making people lazy or by clouding their naturally clear mental vision. Hence, people should rely on their naturally clear faculty of reason when searching for the truth instead of on the authority of an abstruse system of logic.

Another criticism of dialectic important for understanding Descartes' method focuses on the inability of syllogistic reasoning to attain new knowledge:

> But to make it even clearer that [dialectic] contributes nothing whatever to knowledge of the truth, we should realize that, on the basis of their method, dialecticians are unable to formulate a syllogism with a true conclusion unless they are already in possession of the substance of the conclusion, i.e. unless they have previous knowledge of the very truth deduced in the syllogism. (AT X 406: CSM I 36–37)

Descartes' point in this passage is that a syllogism's conclusion does not yield any new knowledge simply because the knowledge of the conclusion is somehow 'contained' in the knowledge of the premises. To help illustrate this point, let's take a look at the following syllogism:

1. All buildings over 300 feet tall are skyscrapers.
2. Some examples of modern architecture are not skyscrapers.
3. Therefore, some examples of modern architecture are not buildings over 300 feet tall.

Notice that premise 1 is a universal claim about all buildings over 300 feet tall, viz. that they fall into the category of things called 'skyscrapers'. On an Aristotelian interpretation, this means that a requirement for being a skyscraper is that it is a building over 300 feet tall. So, to say that some examples of modern architecture are not skyscrapers (i.e. premise 2) is just to say that some examples of modern architecture are not buildings over 300 feet tall (i.e. the conclusion). Accordingly, knowledge of the conclusion is previously known in one of the premises. This example illustrates the point that syllogisms do not yield any new knowledge but simply rehash what was already known. As a result, Descartes believes that they are better suited for explaining what is already known than for discovering new truths (AT VI 17: CSM I 119).

The last of Descartes' criticisms concerns the wide use of probable premises in syllogisms (AT X 363: CSM I 11). If it is only probable or likely that something is true, it follows that there is some chance that it is not true but false. This chance of falsehood allows enough room for the plausibility of other, contrary conclusions. Yet these contrary conclusions could also be false, since they also result from probable syllogisms. Hence, two contrary or even contradictory conclusions *could* each be true (though not both at the same time) but the truth of neither one is established so firmly as to exclude the other from contention. According to Descartes, this mutual plausibility without absolute certainty is what leaves room for controversy and gave rise to many of the disagreements among the learned of his day. Indeed, his concern with the probable or doubtful nature of these syllogisms underscores his profound interest in obtaining indubitable knowledge that would preclude the plausibility of any opposing conclusion, which would, therefore, leave no room for further disagreement.

These criticisms mark out two modern veins in Descartes' thinking that inform his method. The first is that the natural ability to reason is equal in all people and is not the domain of just a few specialists versed in the intricacies of dialectic. In this way, people do not need to rely on the authority of a few specialists, but each person individually can obtain knowledge by using her own natural reasoning abilities. Second, dialectic's uselessness in yielding new knowledge underscores Descartes' modern ideal of scientific progress. That is, he is not satisfied with the rehashing of old knowledge, as were his scholastic-Aristotelian counterparts, but he wanted to discover new truths that would expand scientific knowledge, thereby lessening human toil and making people's lives better. In the end, dialectic is good only for pedagogical purposes in that it does a good job of exercising young minds and explaining what is already known, but it is useless in the search for new knowledge.

1.2 GEOMETRIC METHOD

Descartes' rejection of dialectic means that he needs another method of enquiry in order to carry out his scientific and philosophical projects. In the *Discourse on Method*, Descartes criticizes algebra and geometry as two candidates for this new, non-syllogistic method. A difficulty with both is that they concern very abstract subjects without much practical use. Moreover, geometry's concern for shapes is too tiring for the imagination, which must in some way picture them for a time; and algebra is 'so confined to certain rules and symbols that the end result is a confused and obscure art which encumbers the mind, rather than a science which cultivates it' (AT VI 18: CSM I 119–20). This last criticism echoes his previous one against dialectic in that the variety of rules in algebra hinders the mind from performing its natural activities. So, the methods of geometry and algebra, taken by themselves, cannot constitute a new method that both is simple to use and efficiently pursues new knowledge.

Descartes continues in the following paragraphs of the *Discourse* to explain that his new method should maintain the benefits of logic, geometry and algebra while avoiding their defects. Since one of the main defects of dialectic and algebra is the variety and number of their rules, Descartes proposes only the following four rules for his new method:

1. [N]ever to accept anything as true if I did not have evident knowledge of its truth; that is, carefully to avoid precipitate conclusions and preconceptions, and to include nothing more in my judgments than what presented itself to my mind so clearly and so distinctly that I had no occasion to doubt it.
2. [T]o divide each of the difficulties I examined into as many parts as possible and as may be required in order to resolve them better.
3. [T]o direct my thoughts in an orderly manner, by beginning with the simplest and most easily known objects in order to ascend little by little, step by step, to knowledge of the most complex, and by supposing some order even among objects that have no natural order of precedence.
4. [T]hroughout to make enumerations so complete, and reviews so comprehensive, that I could be sure of leaving nothing out. (AT VI 18–19: CSM I 120)

Here the rules are so few and so simple that they do not 'dim' the natural light of reason; they therefore avoid the defects of dialectic and algebra in his new method.

However, he does want to retain the benefits of mathematical and especially geometrical reasoning, as he explains in the following paragraph:

Those long chains of very simple and easy reasonings, which geometers customarily use to arrive at their most difficult demonstrations, had given me occasion to suppose that all the things which can fall under human knowledge are interconnected in the same way. And I thought that, provided we refrain from accepting anything as true which is not, and always keep to the order required for deducing one thing from another, there can be nothing too remote to be reached in the end or too well hidden to be discovered. (AT VI 19: CSM I 120)

Much of this passage is also expressed in rule 3 of the *Discourse* listed above and makes three general points about the geometric inspiration for Descartes' method. First, geometrical reasoning is the model for the kind of inference he wants to maintain in his more general method. This is because geometrical chains of reasoning are 'very simple' and can be used to demonstrate very difficult theorems. Second, the interconnection of geometric truths led him to suppose that all human knowledge is similarly interconnected. Accordingly, if one were to strictly follow a geometric line of reasoning, making simple inferences from one truth to the next, then there is nothing that is not discoverable by human reason. It just takes patience to move 'little by little, step by step' from one truth to the next, to the next, etc. Third, just as geometry begins with self-evident axioms, so Descartes' method is also supposed to start with the simplest and most easily known truths and from there proceed to more and more complex truths. The geometrical aspects of this method are examined more fully in the remainder of this chapter.

1.3 INTUITION

Now that the complex rules of dialectic have been discarded and replaced by the short set of four geometrically inspired rules from the *Discourse* listed above, the mind can, under their guidance, use its now unhindered natural powers of cognition to discover the truth. The two natural and proper functions of the mind in this endeavour are intuition and deduction. This section will deal exclusively with intuition, and deduction is discussed in the next section.

'Intuition' is the English translation of the Latin *intueri*, which just means 'to look or gaze at'. Hence, Cartesian 'intuition' consists in a mental or intellectual 'look' or 'gaze'. What this implies is that there are some truths that the mind can immediately perceive without the mediation of something else, just like the axioms of geometry. Descartes characterizes intuition a little more precisely in the following way:

By 'intuition' I do not mean the fluctuating testimony of the senses or the deceptive judgment of the imagination as it botches things together but the conception of a clear and attentive mind, which is so easy and distinct that there can be no room for doubt about what we are understanding. Alternatively, and this comes to the same thing, intuition is the indubitable conception of a clear and attentive mind which proceeds solely from the light of reason. (AT X 368: CSM I 14)

According to this passage, intuition occurs when an uncluttered or clear mind directly perceives an indubitable truth. Notice that this perception does not require any previous knowledge, as do the syllogisms of dialectic, but rather it requires only 'the light of reason', which is no longer 'dimmed' by the rules of dialectic, and as such the mind is now 'clear'. It is also important that the mind is 'attentive'; that is, intuition requires that the mind focus or concentrate on its object. This focus or attention is supposed to allow the mind to perceive this object clearly. This point is nicely illustrated by the following example: if one were to try to perceive all the paintings hanging in the National Gallery in a single glance, then she would have only a vague and confused vision of them. Similarly, if she were to spread her mental attention over a variety of different problems, she would maintain only a few confused opinions on various subjects. Indeed, just as it would be better to focus one's sight on each individual painting at the National Gallery in order to gain a clear vision of each one, so it is also better to focus one's mental attention on just one issue at a time.[1]

It is also noteworthy that this intuition of the truth is indubitable, as required by rule 1 of the *Discourse* listed above. The now clear light of reason provides this intuition so that it is impossible for anyone having it to doubt its truth. If someone were to doubt it, then it would be the result of his natural light somehow being dimmed by either a cumbersome method or prior prejudice. The indubitability of intuition also avoids dialectic's defect of promoting controversy. For, unlike probable syllogisms, intuitions are impossible to doubt and so they are absolutely certain. Accordingly, there is no room for denying any of them in favour of some other, contrary position.

Descartes expands on the requirements for intuition in the following excerpt from Rule 11 of the *Regulae*: 'two things are required for mental intuition: first, the proposition intuited must be clear and distinct; second, the whole proposition must be understood all at once, and not bit by bit' (AT X 407: CSM I 37). This doctrine of clear and distinct ideas expressed in the first requirement is an extremely important facet of Descartes' mature thought as expressed in the *Meditations* and the *Principles* and, ironically enough, quite obscure. An in-depth discussion of this notion is not appropriate for the purposes of this chapter but will have to wait until 5.4 below. But suffice it to say for now that a proposition (or idea) is clear when it is in sharp mental focus. A proposition or idea is distinct when it is both clear and sufficiently separated from all other propositions or ideas so that nothing is mixed in with it that would obscure its content.[2]

Yet, in addition to being clear and distinct, the entire proposition 'must be understood all at once, and not bit by bit'. This second requirement indicates that an intuition does not occur piecemeal but in one sweeping mental gaze, which is what makes the operation simple. But what can be understood in such an immediate and almost spontaneous way? Descartes provides some help answering this question with the following examples: 'Thus everyone can mentally intuit that he exists, that he is thinking, that a triangle is bounded by just three lines, and a sphere by a single surface, and the like.' He goes on to mention that '[p]erceptions such as these are more numerous than most people realize, disdaining as they do to turn their minds to such simple matters' (AT X 368: CSM I 14). This latter excerpt indicates not only that most people ignore these kinds of truths but also that Descartes considers those matters just listed to be simple, which is to say that they are not composed of a multiplicity of parts. It is the simplicity of these truths that facilitates the simplicity of the mental operation of intuition itself. Complex truths, i.e. truths composed of parts, require people to focus first on one part and then on another and so on in order for the mind to have a clear and distinct perception of the whole thing. But since simple truths do not have parts, no succession of perceptions is required, but the whole thing can be understood with a single sweep of one's mental gaze and all at once. So, in sum, an intuition in this context is a simple, sweeping gaze of a clear and attentive mind whose indubitable content is illuminated solely by the now undimmed natural light of reason.

1.4 DEDUCTION

Whereas intuition concerns self-evident truths that are perceivable solely by the light of reason, deduction is the mental power everyone has for perceiving the links in a chain of reasoning from intuited self-evident truths, axioms or first principles to those that are more complex. Descartes characterizes deduction as 'the inference of something as following necessarily from some other propositions which are known with certainty' (AT X 369: CSM I 15). The main point is that deduction is the perception of a necessary connection from some absolutely certain proposition to another.

Although it may be easy for us to take this to be a very sharp distinction between intuition and deduction, Descartes is quite careful to note a very close relation between them that actually blurs this line. First, he points out that 'the self-evidence and certainty of intuition is required not only for apprehending single propositions, but also for any train of reasoning whatever' (AT X 369: CSM I 14–15). Hence, the aforementioned necessary connection between absolutely certain propositions is also perceived by intuition; that is, the connection itself is perceived by a simple, sweeping mental gaze. When this occurs in a chain of reasoning, deduction then becomes nothing other than a series of intuitions. So, why make this distinction at all? Descartes gives the following answer:

> But this distinction had to be made, since very many facts which are not self-evident are known with certainty, provided they are inferred from true and known principles through a continuous and uninterrupted movement of thought in which each individual proposition is clearly intuited. (AT X 369: CSM I 15)

An important point made in this passage is that absolutely certain knowledge does not need to be self-evident but can be 'inferred from [other] true and known principles.' So, the absolutely certain knowledge of intuited self-evident truths or propositions can carry over to other propositions so long as the mind intuits a necessary link between them.

Descartes illustrates his point with the following example:

> Take for example, the inference that 2 plus 2 equals 3 plus 1: not only must we intuitively perceive that 2 plus 2 make 4 and that 3 plus 1 make 4, but also that the original proposition follows necessarily from the other two. (AT X 369: CSM I 15)

In this example, notice that $2 + 2 = 4$ and $3 + 1 = 4$ are each intuitively known when we focus our mental attention on one and then on the other. But a further intuition is required for recognizing the necessary connection between these two absolutely certain propositions and the inference to the more complex proposition (i.e. $2 + 2 =$

3 + 1). This third intuition added to the other two is presumably based on the intuited, self-evident principle that two things equal to some third thing are themselves equal. So, in this example, there are three interconnected intuitions that are mentally intuited one after the other in order to achieve absolutely certain knowledge of the conclusion that $2 + 2 = 3 + 1$. Hence, whereas an intuition is an immediate and simple mental perception of some truth, deduction is a series of such mental perceptions one after the other that preserves certainty from proposition to proposition.

This leads to another difference between intuition and deduction as distinguished by Descartes:

> This is similar to the way in which we know that the last link in a long chain is connected to the first: even if we cannot take in at one glance all the intermediate links on which the connection depends, we can have knowledge of the connection provided we survey the links one after the other, and keep in mind that each link from first to last is attached to its neighbour. (AT X 369–70: CSM I 15)

First, this passage reiterates a previous point about intuitions, viz. they are perceived in one mental gaze or glance. However, since deductions are composed of simpler parts, they do not occur all at once but in sequence. Hence, self-evident first principles are known only through intuition, while conclusions reached way down the chain and logically 'far away' from these first principles are known only through deduction. But those conclusions that are drawn immediately from self-evident first principles can be said to be known through deduction in one way and through intuition in another. Insofar as these conclusions are known through an intuition of the necessary connection between it and a first principle, they are known through deduction. But such conclusions are in a sense perceived by intuition in that the entire inference can be perceived in one, sweeping mental glance and all at once, since there are very few links in the chain.

This last point has at least two further implications for Descartes' theory of deduction. First, the greater the number of links in the chain, the more difficult it is to perceive the whole chain all at once and, therefore, the less likely it is to be known through intuition. Second, this view also highlights the very important role of memory in Descartes' account of deduction, for remembering previous links is key to knowing that the chain of inference is not broken. This perception of an unbroken chain of necessary connections from one proposition to another is required for knowing that the remote conclusion is just as indubitable as the self-evident first principles at the beginning of that chain. Since memory is faulty in that we do not always remember things, Descartes wishes to minimize the role of memory in deduction through the procedure of 'enumeration', which is the subject of the next section.

1.5 ENUMERATION

This notion of 'enumeration' is explained in some detail in Rules 7, 10 and 11 of the *Regulae* and is also mentioned in rule 4 of the *Discourse* listed above, which reads: 'Throughout to make enumerations so complete, and reviews so comprehensive, that I could be sure of leaving nothing out.' Moreover, as will be indicated further in later chapters, the notion of enumeration explained in the *Regulae* is prominently at work in the later *Meditations*.[3] Accordingly, this feature of his method is very important for understanding how Descartes reached the conclusions found in his mature works. Understanding the operation of enumeration is difficult and is complicated further by the fact that Descartes wants to use it for at least two distinct purposes. The first is to provide a method for solving complex problems, while the second provides a way for the mind to adequately perceive all the links in a very long deductive chain. Notice that the first application occurs at the beginning of the process, while the second occurs either during a deduction or after it is completed.

It is important to recognize at the outset that the Latin *enumeratio* just means 'list', and so an enumeration is just some kind of listing. However, this is no mere laundry list but an operation 'required for the completion of our knowledge' (AT X 388: CSM I 25). How so? The answer to this question lies in enumeration's two-fold function previously mentioned. The first function 'consists in a thorough investigation of all the points relating to the problem at hand' (AT X 388: CSM I 25). The point is to methodically examine all the possible paths for attaining the correct answer to any problem. This involves ordering all the pertinent elements of a problem so as to ensure that nothing has been inadvertently overlooked. However, the nature of this ordering will depend on the issue at hand and can be a matter of individual choice (see AT X 390–1: CSM I 26–7). This is especially helpful when the problem is very complex, because such an ordered listing would make it easier for the mind to give each possibility the attention it deserves. This ordering, according to Descartes, should be into classes of things due to the impracticality and, in some cases, impossibility of scrutinizing each individual item. This organization into classes is quite evident in Descartes' division of his beliefs into those derived from sensation and those derived from reason in the *First Meditation* and his division of ideas into innate, fabricated and adventitious in the *Third Meditation*.[4] This 'well-devised order' makes it easier to examine a large number of items that may have seemed too large at first (see AT X 391: CSM I 27). Here, at the beginning of the problem-solving process, enumeration is used to make complex problems easier to examine, and maybe even solve, by starting off with an organized list of all the items relevant to the problem at hand.[5]

This organized list of relevant elements can also be seen as a list of hypotheses ordered so that each receives the mental attention it deserves. These hypotheses constitute a list of all the possible causes of a given effect. The aim would then be to examine each hypothesis in order to distinguish which is the real cause of a given effect from those that are not.[6] This use of enumeration is at work in various places in the *Meditations*. Perhaps the most obvious one is in the *Sixth Meditation* where Descartes argues for the existence of material objects existing outside the mind. There he lists the possible causes of the mind's idea of material things, i.e. himself (or the mind itself), material things themselves, God or some creature nobler than a body. Notice that these possible causes are, in some sense, organized into classes or sets. For instance, he considers the possibility of material things themselves without considering each individual material thing. This is also the case with those 'creatures more noble than a body'. The possibility of God is just the set of infinite things, which happens to be a singleton set. And finally, the possibility of the cause of these ideas being 'myself' can be generalized to express the possibility of anything within the set of finite human minds being the cause of its own ideas of material things. Once this organization into classes is complete, Descartes then examines each one, eliminating those that could not possibly be the true cause, until he reaches the conclusion that only material things themselves could possibly be the cause of his ideas of them.[7] But notice that the aim of the enumeration is to facilitate a process of elimination wherein each incorrect item on the list is eliminated until all that remains is the correct answer or cause.

The second function of this operation concerns deductions that have already been completed. Recall from the previous section that some lines of reasoning can be considered deductions in one way but intuitions in another. In these cases, the links in the deductive chain from self-evident first principles to conclusion are so few that the mind can perceive the whole chain in one sweeping mental glance. In fact, Descartes goes on to propose that the mind can be trained to do this with fairly long deductions:

> I shall run through [the links in the deductive chain] several times in a continuous movement of the imagination, simultaneously intuiting one relation and passing on to the next, until I have learnt to pass from the first to the last so swiftly that memory is left with practically no role to play, and I seem to intuit the whole thing at once. (AT X 388: CSM I 25)

Here Descartes exhorts us to go over the chain of reasoning again and again so that we can eventually traverse the entire chain so swiftly that the whole thing *seems* to be perceived all at once. The purpose of this operation is to minimize the need for remembering earlier links in the deductive chain when considering conclusions remote from their initial first principles. Such lines of reasoning are deductions in that they are the result of perceiving necessary connections from first principles, through intermediate conclusions, to a conclusion. But they *seem* to be intuitions in that the movement of thought from first principles to conclusion is so fast that the whole thing *seems* to be perceived all at once.

However, some lines of reasoning are so complex and involved that not even this exercise in mental swiftness can overcome the short-comings of memory. After reiterating how an entire deduction can also be intuited, Descartes explains:

> That is why we are supposing that the deduction is made through intuition when it is simple and transparent but not when it is com-plex and involved. When the latter is the case, we call it 'enumera-tion' or 'induction', since the intellect cannot simultaneously grasp it as a whole and its certainty in a sense depends on memory, which must retain the judgments we have made on the individual parts of the enumeration if we are to derive a single conclusion from them taken as a whole. (AT X 408: CSM I 37)

Here enumeration is characterized as a deduction that is so complex and involved that the whole thing cannot be grasped in one sweeping mental glance. As a result, the conclusion's certainty is jeopardized, because the complexity of the deduction may prevent us from remembering all of its individual links. Under these circumstances, enumeration permits a close scrutiny of each and every link in the deductive chain, which will 'enable us to say that we have seen how the last link is connected with the first' (AT X 389: CSM I 26). But if even the littlest thing is left out, 'the chain is broken and the certainty of the conclusion is entirely lost' (AT X 390: CSM I 26).

Notice that this function of enumeration occurs either during the deduction or after it has taken place. For either an organized list can be made of each and every link in a deductive chain as the mind initially moves from link to link, or it can be made upon the review of a previously completed deductive chain. In either case, the crux is that an ordered list of each of the steps in the argument makes it easier for the mind to scrutinize each and every step in the deduction so as to intuit the necessary connections from link to link, which lowers the likelihood of leaving anything out. This, in turn, fixes the conclusion's certainty, because the series of intuitions constituting the deduction is now understood without any gaps and the mind can perceive how the remote conclusion is connected to initial first principles.

From these considerations, 'enumeration' in general can be characterized in the following way. First, it is a list of items organized in light of the issue at hand and as a matter of personal preference. The main purpose of this organized list is to make it easier for the mind to perceive each and every element and their connections, whether at the beginning, during or at the end of the problem-solving or deductive process. Second, enumeration is necessary for the completion of our knowledge, because it is a process whereby long, complex and involved problems or complex deductions that may at first seem too formidable can be handled and understood in a methodical way.

1.6 ANALYSIS AND SYNTHESIS

The past three sections have examined certain geometrically inspired facets of Descartes' method. First principles or axioms are immediately intuited in a single mental glance from which further necessary connections are intuited one after the other in deductive chains of varying length. Some of these chains are so short that they can be intuited in a single glance, while longer deductive chains can either be gone over so swiftly as to seem to be intuited or are so long that they require an enumeration.

This discovery of simple truths and their use in further deductions is expressed further in what, at the time, were often seen as two parts of the method in geometry, viz. analysis and synthesis. Commentators generally maintain that Descartes borrowed these terms from the widely known discussion of method in geometry by the ancient geometer, Pappus. Some very interesting discussions have arisen in comparing Descartes' use of these terms with Pappus', but at this point such a discussion would lead us too far astray. For now suffice it to say that despite his use of these terms, recent commentary indicates that Descartes departed from Pappus in some important ways.[8]

Traditionally, analysis is a procedure for discovering first principles by starting from the problem and then proceeding until something is reached that is known. The process is reversed in synthesis: the previously discovered first principles are used to reconstruct the problem through a deductive chain, which, in turn, solves the problem. Accordingly, analysis involves breaking down a problem into its constituent parts, while synthesis involves putting that problem back together in light of the discoveries made during analysis. This traditional rendering of analysis and synthesis seems to be expressed in rules 2 and 3 of the *Discourse* as well as in Rule 5 of the *Regulae*:

> We shall be following this method exactly if we first reduce complicated and obscure propositions step by step to simpler ones, and then, starting with the intuition of the simplest ones of all, try to ascend through the same steps to a knowledge of all the rest. (AT X 379: CSM I 20)

However, this quick and easy assimilation of analysis and synthesis with the disassembly and reassembly of propositions quickly runs into problems when applied to the *Meditations*. In the *Second Replies*, Descartes claims that the *Meditations* uses only the method of analysis and not synthesis. Since the *Meditations* is supposed to be a complete metaphysics (leaving nothing out), the method of synthesis is, therefore, not a part of his complete method.

In the section of the *Second Replies* under consideration, Descartes is responding to the suggestion at the end of the *Second Objections* that he lay out his arguments in the 'geometrical fashion', which is to first lay out a series of definitions, axioms and postulates, and then show how various propositions are derived from them in the manner of Euclid (AT VII 128: CSM II 92). Descartes responds by explaining the extent to which the *Meditations* is already written in a geometric fashion. This explanation begins with a distinction between the order and method of demonstration. The *Meditations* follows a geometrical order as defined in the following way:

> The items which are put forward first must be known entirely without the aid of what comes later; and the remaining items must be arranged in such a way that their demonstration depends solely on what has gone before. (AT VII 155: CSM II 110)

This passage indicates that any line of reasoning following this order is 'geometric' to the extent that all its conclusions are based on either first principles or previous conclusions that were ultimately deduced from first principles. But then Descartes continues to make the further distinction between two different methods of demonstration, viz. analysis and synthesis.

Analysis shows how some set of truths was discovered methodically, whereas synthesis demonstrates the conclusion by means of definitions, axioms and postulates. The benefit of synthesis is that if one of the conclusions is denied, it is quite easy to point out how that conclusion is contained in some previous axiom, definition, etc. Although this can allow people to grasp these truths 'in a single glance' and hence even the most argumentative reader would have to agree with it, synthesis is not the best method for those who genuinely want to learn. This more pedagogic purpose is attained in the method of analysis, i.e. the method of discovery (AT VII 156–7: CSM II 110–1). Therefore, even though synthesis has its rhetorical value in quelling argumentative people, Descartes excludes it from his method in favour of the method that shows how some set of truths was discovered.

An interesting feature of this account of the use of synthesis is the fact that argumentative people are compelled to assent to a given conclusion, because 'it can be shown at once that it [the conclusion] is contained in what has gone before' (AT VII 156: CSM II 111). Recall from 1.1 that one reason Descartes rejects the syllogism is that the conclusion is contained in the premises. For Descartes, this amounts to rehashing old knowledge and does not contribute to the discovery of anything new. This is borne out further in that synthesis in geometry was thought to be a follow-up to analysis; hence, whatever truths were contained in the axioms, definitions, etc. of synthesis were previously discovered in analysis. So it is no wonder that Descartes was not too impressed with synthesis, since one of his main goals was to attain new knowledge. Thus, Descartes' mature method can then be understood to be entirely analytic.

The exclusion of synthesis from Descartes' method implies that the dismantling and reassembly of propositions discussed in rules 2 and 3 of the *Discourse* and Rule 5 of the *Regulae* do not correspond to analysis and synthesis respectively but only to analysis. The way this is supposed to work is best explicated through Descartes' metaphor of a house discussed in Part II of the *Discourse* (AT VI 13: CSM I 117). Here Descartes states that just as someone living in a house that is in danger of falling down due to a shaky or weak foundation might tear down his house in order to rebuild it on a more secure foundation, so also his entire system of beliefs is based on an uncertain epistemological foundation and should be torn down and rebuilt on one that is absolutely certain. This corresponds quite nicely with his exhortations to 'divide each of the difficulties I examined into as many parts as possible' and to begin with 'simplest and most easily known objects in order to ascend little by little . . . to knowledge of the most complex' (AT VI 18: CSM I 120). The initial stage of tearing down one's house corresponds to the division of the difficulty into its constituent parts, while rebuilding it on a firmer foundation corresponds to the ascension from the simplest things to the more complex.

The former prong of the method corresponds with the method of analysis as a method of discovery. For the entire point of tearing down his belief system (i.e. his 'house') is to discover an absolutely certain foundation for it. This is borne out nicely in the *Meditations* where Descartes employs the method of doubt (discussed in 1.8) to tear down the old foundations for his beliefs, which then causes the entire system to fall down. He then moves on to discover an absolutely certain first principle (i.e. 'I exist'; see 2.1) from which he is eventually able to discover his absolutely certain epistemological foundation (i.e. that God exists and cannot be a deceiver; see Chapters 4 and 5, respectively). Notice that, in this process, Descartes discovered the simplest truth, viz. that I exist, and then proceeds step by step in a deductive chain to discover his epistemological foundation. From here, he goes on to rebuild his system of beliefs on this more secure foundation. But just as the house that is rebuilt on a new foundation may be the same or different as before, depending on particular features (e.g. its shape and size, etc.) of such a secure foundation, so also the system of beliefs, which is now a system of knowledge (or *scientia*) because of this secure foundation, may be the same or different depending on certain features of the discovered foundation. Hence, the method of analysis for Descartes includes the discovery of the 'rebuilt house' or new system of knowledge that is now based on a new, absolutely certain foundation. In sum, Descartes employs analysis without synthesis in order to discover new truths in such a way as to preserve the geometrical order of reasons where what is first is known without what comes later and what comes later is known only by deducing it from what came before.

1.7 *A PRIORI* AND *A POSTERIORI* DEMONSTRATION

Another issue surrounding Descartes' conception of analysis and synthesis concerns his claim in the *Second Replies* that analysis is 'as it were, *a priori*' whereas synthesis 'employs a directly opposite method where the search is, as it were, *a posteriori* (though the proof itself is often more *a priori* than it is in the analytic method)' (AT VII 156: CSM II 110–11). From a scholastic-Aristotelian perspective, this description of analysis as *a priori* and synthesis as *a posteriori* seems to get it backwards. For them, the term *a posteriori* is supposed to indicate a line of reasoning from effects to their causes, while an *a priori* line of reasoning is supposed to go from cause to effect. Aristotelians believed that scientific enquiry then starts from the phenomenon, which is a perceived effect, and proceeds to an eventual understanding of the phenomenon's previously unknown causes. This line of enquiry is *a posteriori*, because it begins with effects that are by their nature 'posterior' or come after their causes. However, after these causes have been discovered, one can turn around and use them to explain their effects and therefore come to a better understanding of the phenomenon itself.[9]

On this account, an *a posteriori* approach is an enquiry for discovering causes, while an *a priori* approach is an enquiry from causes and how they explain certain effects. Based on this, Descartes' method of analysis should not be *a priori* but *a posteriori*, since it is supposed to be the order of discovery. How are we to make sense of this? Stephen Gaukroger comes up with perhaps the best way of resolving this difficulty. He argues that Descartes has in mind Aristotle's two senses of the terms *a priori* and *a posteriori*. The difference lies in the order of being versus the order of knowledge. Thus, an effect is posterior in being (since it comes after its causes) but prior in knowledge (since effects are often known first and their causes become known only later, after their discovery). But causes are prior in the order of being (since causes exist before their effects) but posterior in the order of knowing (since they are discovered after the perception of the effect).

This helps Gaukroger make sense of Descartes' claims about analysis and synthesis in the *Second Replies*. Analysis is, as it were, *a priori* in that effects are known first, before their causes and the order of discovery is to start with what is already known and then move on to discover new truths. Synthesis, however, is, as it were, *a posteriori* in that it begins from what is known later in the order of discovery, viz. from causes. But a synthetic proof is 'often more *a priori* than it is in the analytic method' in that the initial set of axioms, definitions and postulates are first in the order of being, since these are, in some sense, the causes from which the theorems (i.e. the effects) are deduced.

1.8 THE METHOD OF DOUBT

The last, though certainly not least, feature of Descartes' method to be addressed is his famous method of doubt. This feature of his method is expressed in rule 1 of the *Discourse* where he states that he will 'include nothing more in my judgments than what presented itself to my mind so clearly and so distinctly that I had no occasion to doubt it' (AT VI 18: CSM I 120). Here the general strategy is to cast aside any belief that has even the slightest element of doubt in order to eventually discover some truth or truths that are impossible to doubt in order to render these truths absolutely certain. Although doubt is employed in Part IV of the *Discourse*, Descartes more fully employs it, along with other facets of his method, in his central philosophical work, *Meditations on First Philosophy*.

Descartes' use of doubt is again best illustrated through the image of a house discussed in 1.6. The metaphor of tearing down one's house in order to rebuild it on a new and more secure foundation illustrates Descartes' overall project of tearing down his system of beliefs in order to rebuild it on an absolutely certain epistemological foundation. It is by means of doubt that Descartes carries out the first task of this project: doubt is the wrecking-ball by which he tears down his entire system of beliefs in the beginning of Part IV of the *Discourse* and in the *First Meditation*. In carrying out the destructive side of his project, Descartes is also, to some extent, following rule 3 of the *Discourse* and the first part of Rule 5 of the *Regulae* in that clearing his mind of all doubtful beliefs will allow him to focus on the most simple absolutely certain truths and then allow him to work his way little-by-little to more complex absolutely certain truths. The remainder of this section is devoted to an exposition of this phase of Descartes' project in his mature works.

How doubt is to be used to tear down one's system of beliefs is explained in the following passage from the *First Meditation*:

> Reason now leads me to think that I should hold back my assent from opinions which are not completely certain and indubitable just as carefully as I do from those which are patently false. So, for the purpose of rejecting all my opinions, it will be enough if I find in each of them at least some reason for doubt. And to do this I will not need to run through them all individually, which would be an endless task. Once the foundations of a building are undermined, anything built on them collapses of its own accord; so I will go straight for the basic principles on which all my former beliefs rested. (AT VII 18: CSM II 12)

It is evident from this passage that the destruction of all of the Meditator's beliefs will consist in not assenting to anything with even the slightest hint of doubt.[10] This is taken a step further by the Meditator's pronouncement that he will consider such doubtful beliefs false.[11] The next step in the process is then to determine which of his beliefs are doubtful and which are absolutely certain. The Meditator does not plan on running through all of his beliefs one by one in order to accomplish this task. Instead, he directs his efforts to the principles or foundations upon which those beliefs are based. If he can consider the foundations of his beliefs false, because they are doubtful, then the beliefs resting on them will fall all by themselves. In effect, the Meditator, in accordance with rule 4 of the *Discourse*, enumerates his beliefs into two categories, viz. those based on sensation and those based on mathematical reasoning, and then proceeds to show how each set of beliefs is based on doubtful foundations.

Doubt is raised about these two classes of beliefs through the use of scenarios commonly employed by some of the ancient Sceptics.[12] The thrust of these scenarios is to provide a more or less plausible causal explanation of how someone could come to have a set of beliefs that she thinks are true but are really false.[13] The Meditator's first targets are those beliefs based on sensory experience. He begins his assault with the mundane observation that the senses sometimes deceive us. The point is that some things are presented by the senses as being quite small when in fact they are quite large. They just appear small because they are being seen at a distance. So the senses should not be trusted, because it is not prudent to trust anyone who has deceived us even once (AT VII 18: CSM II 12). This raises suspicions about the reliability of sense perceptions, which are often thought to be the most reliable – after all, it is often said that we 'have to see it to believe it'.

Although this sheds doubt on a few sorts of sensory beliefs, like things viewed at a distance, other sensory beliefs are not called into doubt on this account, 'for example, that I am here, sitting by the fire, wearing a winter dressing gown, holding this piece of paper in my hands, and so on' (AT VII 18: CSM II 13). Hence, the unreliability of the senses does not call into doubt our beliefs based on the immediate sense perception of what is happening right here and now. But maybe the brain is 'so damaged by the persistent vapours of melancholia' that these beliefs based on immediate sense perception are the delusions of a madman. Indeed, madmen sometimes sincerely believe they are made of glass or that they are kings when they are paupers. So, what prevents the belief that one is, for instance, reading this book from being caused by such 'persistent vapours' in the brain akin to those that cause people to believe they are made of glass? The Meditator's only response to this question is that he 'would be thought equally mad if [he] took anything from them as a model for [him]self' (AT VII 19: CSM II 13). This indicates that madness is not a sufficient reason for doubting his sensory beliefs, because this scenario undermines his own rationality. In other words, beliefs held by madmen are by their nature irrational, but this enquiry requires a rational Meditator in order to follow the geometrical order of this analytic demonstration. So, madness is not a sufficient reason for doubt, for that would then undermine the entire project

However, sane, rational people often believe that such fantastic falsehoods are true when they are dreaming. This is because the sensory images found in dreams are not real sensations caused by actual physical objects but mere fictions of the mind. That is, the mind presents us with images that we often believe to be the result of the interaction of our sense organs with physical objects when in fact they result from our own imagination. Moreover, dreams do not need to be fantastic but can concern the most ordinary experiences:

> Yet at the moment my eyes are certainly wide awake when I look at this piece of paper; I shake my head and it is not asleep; as I stretch out and feel my hand I do so deliberately, and I know what

I am doing. All this would not happen with such distinctness to someone asleep. Indeed! As if I did not remember other occasions when I have been tricked by exactly similar thoughts while asleep! . . . I see plainly that there are never any sure signs by means of which being awake can be distinguished from being asleep. (AT VII 19: CSM II 13)

Thus, there is no way of being certain that one is awake and not sleeping. Accordingly, sensory experiences could seem true but really be false to him, because he is not really 'looking at this piece of paper' but is 'undressed and in bed'. Hence, the inability to distinguish waking life from a dream raises the possibility that there are no true sensory experiences but only the false images of dreams. This scenario then explains how someone might be caused to believe that the beliefs based on the sensation are true when in fact they are false. This, in turn, raises doubt about all such sensory beliefs, including those composing the natural sciences like physics, astronomy and medicine (AT VII 20: CSM II 14). Since this set of beliefs has been found doubtful, the Meditator can now consider them all false for the sake of his method. So, all beliefs based on sensation have now been destroyed by doubt.

Yet, although the dreaming scenario casts doubt on beliefs based on sensation, it does not affect those based on mathematical reasoning. 'For whether I am awake or asleep, two and three added together are five, and a square has no more than four sides' (AT VII 20: CSM II 14). Thus the Meditator needs some other likely story to explain why he believes such simple mathematical beliefs are true when in fact they are false. The scenario for calling these beliefs into doubt begins with the belief that there is a God that made him as he is and that he has no way to tell whether or not God is deceiving him so that he believes the earth, the sky and material things extend in three dimensions, and their size, shape and location exist when in fact they do not. Accordingly, beliefs based on sensation are hit with two scenarios for doubt: one being the dream argument and the other the possibility that God is deceiving him so that he is automatically mistaken about the existence of physical objects.

The Meditator then observes that people sometimes make mistakes when making even the simplest mathematical calculations. But again the same considerations about God deceiving him about material things can also be applied to mathematical beliefs: 'may I not similarly go wrong every time I add two and three or count the sides of a square or in some even simpler matter, if that is imaginable?' (AT VII 21: CSM II 14). The point is that maybe God has made him in such a way that he is always mistaken when he adds two and three. If that is the case, then even such simple mathematical beliefs are doubtful and, therefore, he can consider them false as well.

This reason for doubt is strengthened by those who would rather deny the existence of such an all-powerful God. For these people must account for their existence in some way, whether by fate or chance or a continuous chain of events or in some other way, 'yet since deception and error seem to be imperfections, the less powerful they make my original cause, the more likely it is that I am so imperfect as to be deceived all the time' (AT VII 21: CSM II 14). So, fate, chance or a continuous chain of events would be a much less perfect cause of the Meditator's existence than an all-powerful God, and as such the imperfection of his origin implies even further imperfection in himself. Under these circumstances he would be even more likely to be mistaken all the time about such simple things as two plus three equalling five. And so all beliefs based on sensation and on mathematics are still called into doubt even if there is no God at all (let alone a deceiving god) and the Meditator can, therefore, consider them false.

So, by the end of the *First Meditation*, the Meditator considers false all beliefs based on sensation and mathematical reasoning, because the dream argument and the deceiving God scenario have shown that all such beliefs have some element of doubt about them. He has, at this point, torn down his 'house' or system of beliefs, which serves to clear his mind of any previous opinions he might have so that he can intuit anything that is immune from these scenarios for doubt if such a truth exists at all. Hence, at the beginning of the *Second Meditation*, the Meditator claims that: 'It feels as if I have fallen unexpectedly into a deep whirlpool which tumbles me around so that I can neither stand on the bottom nor swim up to the top' (AT VII 24: CSM II 16). Perhaps the one thing that is certain is that nothing is certain. All he needs now is a foothold from which he can extricate himself from these doubts. The Meditator's discovery of this foothold begins the next chapter.

CHAPTER 2

MIND AND IDEA

The initial seed of Descartes' philosophical tree is the famous dictum, 'I think, therefore I am.' For just as the roots of a tree are the first to sprout from a seed, so the roots of Descartes' philosophy, i.e. his metaphysics, also sprout directly from this ultimate first principle. This chapter begins with a look at how the conclusion 'I am' is derived from his methodological doubt. Attention is then given to the thinking nature of Descartes' 'I' or self and his enumeration of the kinds of ideas this 'I' can possess.

2.1 'I THINK, THEREFORE I AM'

Recall from the previous chapter that after the radical doubts discussed at the beginning of Part IV of the *Discourse* and in the *First Meditation*, Descartes and the Meditator, respectively, find themselves spinning around in a whirlpool of false beliefs. The question then arises: What, if anything, is absolutely certain? Ironically enough, the answer to this question is found in the very fact that he is doubting. As Janet Broughton has convincingly argued, the later results of the *Meditations* are necessary conditions for the possibility of doubting in the first place. The fact that this is Descartes' strategy is evident in a letter dated April or May 1638 in response to some queries made about the *Discourse* by his long time friend and gentleman-in-waiting to the Prince of Orange, Alphonse Pollot:

> Although the Pyrronhists[1] reached no certain conclusions from their doubts, it does not follow that no one can, I would try now to show how these doubts can be used to prove God's existence ... (AT II 38–9: CSM K 99)

This is repeated in the unpublished, metaphysical dialogue, *Search for Truth*, through the character of Eudoxus who is commonly considered Descartes' mouthpiece:

> Just give me your attention and I shall conduct you further than you think. For from this universal doubt, as from a fixed and immovable point, I propose to derive the knowledge of God, of yourself and of everything in the universe. (AT X 515: CSM II 409)

Here, Descartes claims to turn sceptical arguments against themselves in that the doubt they generate presupposes other truths that are themselves immune from doubt. Hence, Descartes' strategy is to start from the existence of doubt and then search for conditions that must be satisfied in order for this doubt even to be possible.[2] According to the excerpt from the *Search for Truth*, this will result in knowledge of everything in the universe.

The use of doubt as the immovable point from knowledge of the self is obtained and 'I think, therefore I am' is discovered. In the *Discourse*, Descartes claims to discover this immediately upon calling everything into doubt (AT VI 32: CSM I 127). In the *Meditations*, the Meditator reasons that 'I am, I exist' is necessarily true, because even if he is dreaming or being deceived by some god, there must be an 'I' or a self (i.e. himself) that is doing the dreaming or undergoing the deception (AT VII 25: CSM II 17). However, an interesting and important point of difference between the *Discourse* and the *Meditations* is that the formula 'I think, therefore I am' is excluded from the latter in favour of merely 'I am, I exist.'[3] The 'therefore' in the first formulation indicates that 'I am' is a conclusion deduced from 'I think.' But the absence of 'therefore' from the formulation found in the *Meditations* implies that it is an intuition. So which is it?

Before answering this question, it is important to understand how 'I exist' is a necessary precondition for the possibility of doubt. This is perhaps most readily apparent in Eudoxus' explanation of it to Polyander in the *Search for Truth*:

> You [Polyander] cannot deny that you have such doubts; rather it is certain that you have them, so certain in fact that you cannot doubt your doubting. Therefore, it is also true that you who are doubting exist; this is so true that you can no longer have any doubts about it. (AT X 515: CSM II 409–10)

In this passage, Descartes (through Eudoxus) makes it clear that one's own existence can be deduced with absolute certainty from the certitude of the fact that one is doubting. Hence, my existence is a necessary condition for my ability to doubt, and accordingly the existence of doubt implies the existence of the self or an 'I' who is doing the doubting.

Descartes makes another logical point about this at *Principles* I.7:

> But we cannot for all that suppose that we, who are having such thoughts, are nothing. For it is a contradiction to suppose that what thinks does not, at that very time when it is thinking, exist. Accordingly, the piece of knowledge – *I am thinking, therefore I exist* – is the first and most certain of all to occur to anyone who philosophizes in an orderly way. (AT VIIIA 7: CSM I 194–5)

In this passage, the logical notion of contradiction takes centre-stage. Descartes' line of reasoning here goes something like this: Let us suppose that (1) I am now thinking and (2) I do not now exist. But if I am now thinking, then I must also now exist, because any activity occurring right now (e.g. thinking) requires an actor (e.g. a thinker) to perform it at that time. Therefore, since it has already been supposed that I am now thinking, it follows that I must now also exist. But this contradicts the second supposition that I do not now exist. Therefore, the supposition that (1) I am now thinking and (2) I do not now exist is self-contradictory. Hence, the fact that I exist is not only a necessary condition for the possibility of doubt, but it is also self-contradictory to suppose that there is doubting or thinking occurring without a doubter or thinker to perform the activity.[4] As a result, 'I think, therefore I am' is self-justified because its falsehood cannot be supposed without contradiction.

This leads back to the question about the nature of Descartes' discovery: is it an intuition or a deduction? The short answer is that it is both. The issue arises from the formulation of the proposition itself. The 'therefore' in 'I think, therefore I am' indicates that 'I am' or 'I exist' is a deductive consequence resulting from the fact that 'I think', and so it appears to be a deduction. However, Descartes seems to deny this in the following excerpt from the *Second Replies*:

> When someone says 'I am thinking, therefore I am, or I exist', he does not deduce existence from thought by means of a syllogism, but recognizes it as something self evident by a simple intuition of the mind. (AT VII 140: CSM II 100)

In this passage, Descartes describes 'I think, therefore I am' as being perceived or 'recognized' by a simple intuition, and therefore it is a self-evident truth that does not result from deduction. Accordingly, this proposition is an intuited first principle from which other truths can be deduced.

But notice that he also claims that it is not a deduction 'by means of a syllogism'. This does not mean that it is not a deduction at all but only that the deduction is not syllogistic. The reason for this can be explained by the context of Descartes' reply. Here Descartes is responding to a concern raised in the *Second Objections*. This issue pertains to the claim that the Meditator cannot have knowledge until he knows that God exists and cannot be a deceiver, which occurs in the *Third* and *Fourth Meditations* respectively.[5] Hence, in order for the Meditator to deduce his existence from his thinking in the *Second Meditation*, it seems that he should have prior knowledge of the fact that he is a thinking thing. But since he is not entitled to any prior knowledge at that point given the geometrical order of the *Meditations*, it seems to follow that the Meditator cannot know that he exists before knowing that God exists without violating the geometrical order.

Descartes' claim that no prior knowledge is required for knowing with absolute certainty that 'I exist' harks back to his criticism of dialectic or syllogistic logic discussed in Chapter 1.1. Recall that one of Descartes' complaints about the syllogism is that it does nothing but rehash what is already known. Such previous knowledge would upset the geometrical order of the *Meditations*, and therefore the structure of the *Meditations* itself precludes syllogistic reasoning altogether. But yet Descartes concedes that some prior knowledge is required. At *Principles* I.10, Descartes states that 'I think, therefore I am' does require that 'one must first know what thought, existence and certainty are, and that it is impossible that that which thinks should not exist and so forth' (AT VIIIA 8: CSM I 196). However, Descartes continues on to claim that notions such as thought, existence and certainty are so simple that they require no further definition (AT VIIIA 8: CSM I 196). The simplicity of these notions indicates further that their perception is a matter of intuition. Their individual simplicity and their relation as expressed in 'I think, therefore I am or I exist' indicates further that there is a deduction at work here but just not a syllogistic one.

Now, recall from Chapter 1.4 that short deductions can also be intuited. 'I think, therefore I am' is a deduction, because it expresses a chain of intuitively grasped truths. 'I think' is grasped in a single mental glance as is its necessary connection to 'I am or I exist' based on the more general, intuitively known principle that the occurrence of any activity (e.g. thinking) requires the existence of an actor (e.g. a thinker). Therefore, 'I think, therefore I am' expresses a deductive chain between 'I think' and 'I am'. But this deductive chain is so short that it can be intuited in a single mental glance, and so it is, to this extent, an intuition.

In sum, 'I think, therefore I am' expresses a deduction so simple that it can be intuited all at once in a single, sweeping mental glance, and therefore it is both a deduction and an intuition as discussed above. Moreover, the existence of an 'I' who thinks is a necessary condition for the possibility of doubting in the first place, because there must be a doubter or thinker in order for the activities of doubting or thinking to occur, and therefore 'I am' or 'I exist' is absolutely certain despite such hyperbolic doubts. As a result, 'I think, therefore I am' is the self-evident first principle of Descartes' philosophy and, therefore, it provides the starting point for intuiting or deducing other, absolutely certain truths in geometrical order.

2.2 WHAT AM I?

Once the primary truth 'I exist' is established, the question 'What am I?' is posed.[6] The natural response to this question is that 'I am a man'. But what is a man? The standard scholastic-Aristotelian response would be a rational animal. The Meditator quickly dismisses this answer, 'for then I should have to inquire what an animal is, what rationality is, and in this way one question would lead me down the slope to other harder ones' (AT VII 25: CSM II 17) And, 'like the branches of a family tree, [these questions] would rapidly increase and multiply' (AT X 516: CSM II 410). These concerns underscore Descartes' distaste for how the scholastic-Aristotelian manner of philosophizing does not solve problems but makes them more obscure. So, instead of examining this traditional definition of 'what I am', the Meditator decides to examine what comes to him naturally and spontaneously, i.e. intuitively. What comes to him first is that he is that mechanical configuration of limbs called 'the body'. The second is that he was nourished, moved about, and engaged in sense perception and thinking, which he attributed to the soul (AT VII 25-6: CSM II 17). So, in this initial enumeration of the possible answers to this question, the Meditator previously thought he was some kind of combination of soul and body.

Once this enumeration is complete, the Meditator proceeds with an examination of his notion of the body:

> whatever has a determinable shape and a definable location and can occupy a space in such a way as to exclude any other body; it can be perceived by touch, sight, hearing, taste or smell, and can be moved in various ways, not by itself but by whatever else comes into contact with it. (AT VII 26: CSM II 17)

Notice that the Meditator judges that self-movement, along with sensation and thought, are entirely alien to the nature of body. In other words, bodies are by their nature inert and as such they cannot move themselves, sense or think. This implies further that the 'I' cannot be a body, even something 'tenuous, like a wind or fire or ether, which permeated my more solid parts' (AT VII 26: CSM II 17). Whereas this conclusion is reached in the *Meditations* by mere inspection of the notions involved, the same point is made using the method of doubt in the *Discourse*. There Descartes points out that even though he cannot doubt that 'I exist', the existence of bodies is still doubtful. It can be deduced from this that 'I' am not a body since its existence is absolutely certain while the existence of bodies is not. This serves to define 'I' negatively as a non-bodily or immaterial thing.[7]

Now that the possibility of him being a body has been eliminated, the Meditator goes on to examine his notion of the soul. He again enumerates the various features he used to ascribe to the soul, such as nutrition, self-movement, sensation and thinking and proceeds by process of elimination to the conclusion that he is nothing but a thinking thing. Upon inspection, it is quite clear that self-movement requires a body that can be moved, and both nutrition and sensation require bodily organs (e.g. stomachs, eyes, etc.) in order to occur. However, since 'I' cannot be a body, it follows that there is no body for 'me' to move or organs by which 'I' can provide myself with nutrition or have sensations. Accordingly, 'I' cannot be any of these things, since 'I' am not a body. Therefore, the only remaining option is that 'I' am a thinking thing:

> [T]hought; this alone is inseparable from me. I am, I exist – that is certain. But for how long? For as long as I am thinking. For it

could be that were I totally to cease from thinking, I should totally cease to exist. (AT VII 27: CSM II 18)

This passage shows that the nature of this 'I', or any self for that matter, is an immaterial thinking thing, i.e. 'a mind, or intelligence, or intellect, or reason' (AT VII 27: CSM II 18). So then, what is thought?

2.3 THOUGHT

In the *Principles*, Descartes defines thought as 'everything which we are aware of as happening within us, in so far as we have awareness of it' (AT VIIIA 7: CSM I 195). He continues on to provide an enumeration of certain kinds of thoughts such as understanding, willing, imagining and also sense perception and doubt. Affirming and denying are also part of the list given in the *Second Meditation* (AT VII 28: CSM II 19). These different species of thought are discussed in this section of the present work.

Descartes divides thought into two general kinds and their sub-species at *Principles* I.32:

All the modes of thinking that we experience within ourselves can be brought under two general headings: perception, or the operation of the intellect, and volition, or the operation of the will. Sensory perception, imagination and pure understanding are simply various modes of perception; desire, aversion, assertion, denial and doubt are various modes of willing. (AT VIIIA 17: CSM I 204)[8]

According to this passage, the two main species of thought are perception (i.e. intellectual operations) and volition (i.e. operations of the will). Each of these faculties then engages in the following various kinds of activities.

Descartes, with regards to the first genus of thought, takes advantage of a certain ambiguity in the Latin *percipere* (commonly translated as 'to perceive') in making this enumeration. This ambiguity lies in its initial meaning of 'to lay hold of or to seize'. This 'taking hold of' can occur either mentally, emotionally or with the senses. Hence, *percipere* can be translated as 'to understand' or 'to sense'. So, sensation, imagination and pure understanding are all a kind of mental 'taking hold' or 'seizing' of some object. For instance, in the case of the images found in sensation or imagination, the mind takes hold of the characteristics of some object, e.g. a tree, insofar as that object exists in the mind. However, unlike sensations and imagining, pure understanding does not require an image in order to take hold of its object. This permits the 'perception' of immaterial objects, like the mind and God, which imagination and sensation only obscure. Hence, all of these perceptions or intellectual operations involve an apprehension (whether clear or obscure) of some object.

At this point the reader may be struck by the inclusion of sensation in the enumeration of mental operations given the Meditator's previous rejection of them when deciding just what he is. Recall that sensation was rejected because sense organs, like eyes and ears, are necessary for it to take place. So, how can sensation be a kind of thinking when the existence of bodies themselves is still in doubt? This latter concern, however, is addressed a little later in the *Second Meditation*:

> For example, I am now seeing light, hearing a noise, feeling heat. But I am asleep, so all this is false. Yet I certainly *seem* to see, to hear, and to be warmed. This cannot be false; what is called 'having a sensory perception' is strictly just this, and in this restricted sense of the term it is simply thinking. (AT VII 29: CSM II 19)

This account of sensation as thinking harks back to the quotation where a thought is just the awareness of something happening within the mind. In the case of dreaming, for example, the dreamer has a sensory perception insofar as he immediately seizes upon an image occurring within him. Whether or not that image was caused by real objects existing outside the mind or is a mere product of the imagination is irrelevant at this point. All that matters is that the thinker has an immediate awareness of an image of a physical thing. Therefore, the mere fact that the Meditator is having an immediate awareness of some object, even though the object itself is not really there, means that he is having a sense perception in a restricted sense.[9] Hence, sensation is a thought insofar as it is constituted by an immediate awareness of a mental image. This is a weak or restricted conception of sensation intended to include false sensations like dreams and hallucinations, whereas the strong conception requires a physical object and the organ appropriate for that kind of sensation, e.g. you need an ear to hear sound, etc. This stronger version of sensation is discussed further at 8.1 and 8.2.

The next genus of thought is volition, which is just an operation of the will, i.e. the faculty of free choice. The point is that the mind chooses what it desires, asserts, avers, denies and doubts. The mind's ability to choose its desires is especially apparent in the third maxim of the *Discourse*'s provisional moral code where he decides to 'change [his] desires rather than the order of the world' (AT VI 25: CSM I 123). Here the main thrust is that only desires and not the order of the world are entirely within people's power. As such, Descartes continues, if failure occurs after doing everything within one's power to achieve some goal, then one ought to consider its achievement impossible, and therefore that goal should no longer be desired, rather than trying to vainly bend the world to one's desire.[10] Part IV of the *Discourse* and the *First Meditation* discussed in Chapter 1.8 are also clear examples of how people can choose to deny beliefs because of even the slightest doubt. In the end, volitions, or operations of the will, are the various ways in which people voluntarily choose to do one thing rather than another. Accordingly, the will is a principle of self-movement impelling people in one direction rather than another, whether literally in the sense of moving their legs to go to the shops or in the more metaphorical sense of 'moving' them to desire something or not, or even morally in the choices they make to pursue or avoid something.

So far intellect (i.e. perceptions) and will (i.e. volitions) are the fundamental operations of a thinking thing for Descartes. However, another secondary faculty is derived from their interaction. This is the faculty of judgement. The Meditator discusses judgement in the *Fourth Meditation* in his attempt to explain why errors occur. Although the account of error will have to wait until 5.4, a brief explanation of judgement can be attempted here. Judgement boils down to the choice to affirm or deny something that is understood. So, then, something must first be perceived by the intellect and then, based on that perception, the will chooses whether to affirm or deny it. Hence, since the faculty of judgement results from the interaction between these two basic kinds of thought, it is a kind of thought as well.

This section has briefly discussed one of the basic operations of a thinking thing, mind or soul for Descartes. However, it is important to bear in mind that these are all operations of pure thought; that is, the mind has these powers regardless of whether or not it is united with a body. Other operations, such as (strong) sensations, like hunger, thirst, pain, and veridical images of physical objects presented to sense organs are also thoughts but only insofar as the mind is united to the body. What this means and how it is supposed to work will be discussed in Chapters 7 and 8.

2.4 IDEAS

Descartes uses the word 'idea' equivocally to refer to both the object of a given thought and an act of thinking (AT VII 8: CSM II 7). For instance, in the case of a child imagining a unicorn, the imagining is a thought or an act of thinking, while the unicorn is the object or content of that thought. But since all ideas have an object, the term 'idea' is strictly applied only to the object or image (AT VII 37: CSM II 25). But even though all ideas have an object (i.e. all ideas are *about* something), others have 'various additional forms: thus when I will, or am afraid, or affirm or deny, there is always a particular thing which I take as the object of my thought, but my thought includes something more than the likeness of that thing' (AT VII 37: CSM II 26). So, 'ideas' in this second sense are just *acts* of thinking, regardless of their object. These ideas include 'thoughts' like imaginings, understandings or perceptions, volitions, emotions and judgments as discussed above.

What that idea represents is what Descartes calls its 'objective reality'. In the *First Replies*, Descartes explains that objective reality or 'being' is just the object itself as it exists in the intellect. For example, a stone or the sun exists in the mind when someone has the idea of them though not actually or literally but 'in the way in which its objects are normally there' (AT VII 102: CSM II 75). Moreover, even though an object's existence in the mind as the objective content of one of its ideas is 'less perfect than that possessed by things which exist outside the intellect', it is still something. Hence, an idea's representational content is not merely nothing but is that object as it exists in the mind in an albeit less real (but not unreal) form. Also, an idea's object or content need not be pictorial but could be of something that could never be perceived by any of the five senses such as the soul or God.

In addition to classifying his ideas by kinds of thinking activity and by their objective content, the Meditator goes on to classify them based on the origin or cause of their existence. These three classes are: innate, adventitious, and fabricated. Innate ideas are those found in his own nature such as 'what a thing is, what truth is, and what thought is', and even though they can be brought before the mind or dismissed at will, their content cannot be changed. For example, someone can think about a triangle when studying geometry and put it aside when it's time to study French, but the triangle that object-ively exists in the idea itself cannot be altered in any way. Adventitious ideas are caused by things located externally to the mind such as seeing the sun or feeling the fire. These ideas are not subject to the will, for 'I notice them even when I do not want to: now, for example, I feel the heat whether I want to or not, and this is why I think that this sensation or idea of heat comes to me from something other than myself' (AT VII 38: CSM II 26). Finally, fabricated or invented ideas, like those of sirens, hippogriffs, etc., are mere inventions since they can be brought before the mind or dismissed at will and their content can be manipulated. These two distinctions between the act and object of thinking as well as the division of these acts into these three categories are important, because they lay the groundwork for the causal arguments for God's existence found in the *Third Meditation* discussed at 4.2 and his proof of a material world in the *Sixth Meditation* discussed at 5.6.

2.5 THE MIND OR SOUL

The nature of the 'I' that exists can be summed up as an immaterial thinking thing or mind with the faculties of intellect (perception) and will (volition). Interestingly enough, Descartes' use of 'mind' here was somewhat novel for the time. Most Aristotelian-scholastic philosophers argued that the mind is merely the rational part of the human soul. But for Descartes, the mind is the human soul in its entirety (AT VII 356: CSM II 246). In the *Fifth Objections*, a leading seventeenth-century proponent of Atomism, and Descartes' rival, Pierre Gassendi raised an interesting question about this conception of the soul:

I was still in doubt about whether you preferred not to use the word 'soul' to apply to the principle responsible for the vegetative and sensory functions in both us and the brutes, but wanted instead to say that the soul in the strict sense was our mind. But since it is the vegetative and sensitive principle that is properly speaking said to 'animate' us ... (AT VII 263: CSM II 184)

In this passage, Gassendi's 'doubt' is with the extent to which Descartes considers the mind to be identical with the soul. This issue stems from the common, Aristotelian understanding of the soul as a principle of life. On this account, every living thing has a soul. For instance, plants are living things insofar as they can provide for their own nutrition and, therefore, a plant soul has just this faculty (what Gassendi calls the 'vegetative function'). Now, animals are also living things that not only provide for their own nutrition but can also have sensations. So, an animal soul has both nutritive (vegetative) and sensory functions. Finally, humans are living things that not only provide for their own nutrition and have sensations, but they also have the ability to think. Accordingly, human souls were thought to contain nutritive, sensory and rational faculties. Hence, Gassendi's concern stems from the absence of the nutritive and sensory faculties from the Meditator's conclusion that he is only a thinking thing, because it leaves out those very faculties by which we consider ourselves and other things, like trees and dogs, animate or alive.

Descartes attempts to clear up this issue in the following passage from the *Fifth Replies*:

> I, by contrast, realizing that the principle by which we are nourished is wholly different – different in kind – from that in virtue of which we think, have said that the term 'soul', when it is used to refer to both these principles, is ambiguous. If we are to take 'soul' in its special sense, as meaning the 'first actuality' or 'principal form of man', then the term must be understood to apply only to the principle in virtue of which we think; and to avoid ambiguity I have as far as possible used the term 'mind' for this. (AT VII 356: CSM II 246)

Although much is going on in this passage, for present purposes it is important to note Descartes' claim that the term 'soul' is ambiguous. Unfortunately, he is not very clear as to where this ambiguity lies. The point seems to be that nutrition and sensation are 'souls' in one sense of the term while the mind is a 'soul' in another sense. The mind is a 'soul' in that it is the 'principal form of man'. This means that Descartes reserves the term 'mind' for that principle that makes something a human being, viz. thinking. Recall that this is an immaterial substance that, as will be discussed in Chapter 7, has the ability to exist without a body. However, in relation to the brutes or animals, the term 'soul' refers to the material principles by which animals are able to nourish themselves and have sensations.

This last statement is substantiated by Descartes' claims in Part V of the *Discourse* where he explicitly deals with the difference between 'men and beasts'. There he argues that the ability to use language is a sign of rationality. So, since animals cannot use language, they are not rational. This means that an immaterial thinking thing or rational soul is not part of the constitution of an animal, but rather 'it is nature which acts in them according to the disposition of their organs' (AT VI 59: CSM I 141). The point is that animal bodies are machines that operate according to the disposition and motion of their parts. So, the nutritive and sensitive faculties normally ascribed to the soul are accounted for here by means of the configuration and motion of material parts. Indeed, these functions are explained in the same manner in human bodies since the human mind or soul is nothing but a thinking thing. So, for Descartes, animals do not have immaterial principles of life (i.e. souls) but only material ones.[11] So, presumably, the term 'soul' can be used to refer to these material principles in animals in some way. But this is quite different than its use when applied to 'the principal form of man', i.e. immaterial thinking things. In the end, Descartes' mind is just the human soul.

2.6 THE MIND IS BETTER KNOWN THAN THE BODY

The full title of the *Second Meditation* is 'The nature of the human mind, and how it is better known than the body' (AT VII 24: CSM II 16). So far sections 2.2 and 2.5 have discussed the nature of the human mind. But another important thesis of this meditation is that the mind is 'better known than the body'. What does this mean and what is its significance? The motivation for making this claim is to undermine the commonsense view that things we see, hear, touch, taste or smell are better or more easily known than those things we can perceive or understand by the mind alone, such as the soul and God.

To make this point, the Meditator takes a 'time-out' from the *Meditations* in order to examine his sensory perceptions of a particular body and show that the mind is better known than this or any body. He uses a piece of wax to illustrate his point:

> Let us take, for example, this piece of wax. It has just been taken from the honeycomb; it has not yet quite lost the taste of honey; it retains some of the scent of the flowers from which it was

gathered; its colour, shape, and size are plain to see, it is hard, cold and can be handled without difficulty; if you rap it with your knuckle it makes a sound. In short, it has everything which appears necessary to enable a body to be known as distinctly as possible. (AT VII 30: CSM II 20)

Notice that the Meditator's description picks out those qualities of the wax that are perceivable by the five senses. But when he moves the wax closer to the fire, all these sensible qualities disappear and are replaced by others, 'the residual taste is eliminated, the smell goes away, the colour changes, the shape is lost, the size increases; it becomes liquid and hot; you can hardly touch it, and if you strike it, it no longer makes a sound' (AT VII 30: CSM II 20). So, what once tasted like honey and smelled like flowers no longer has any discernable taste or odour; the wax has grown in size; and what was once cold and hard is now hot and soft. Accordingly, the wax appears one way to the senses before being moved by the fire and then appears completely different afterwards.

So, even though all of the wax's sensible qualities have changed, we still judge that the melting wax is the same piece of wax as before. But how is this judgment made? Three possible answers are enumerated: sensation, imagination or the mind alone. It cannot be made based on the wax's sensible qualities, because those qualities have completely changed. So, sensation is ruled out as the faculty by which the wax is known. The next possibility is that it is known by the imagination, which is also ruled out because innumerable sizes, shapes and other changes can be imagined. Thus the possibility of even more variation makes it even harder to judge that this is the same piece of wax now as before. Finally, the only remaining option is that the wax itself is perceived by the mind alone (AT VII 31: CSM II 21). The Meditator explains his point thus:

And yet, and here is the point, the perception I have of it is a case not of vision or touch or imagination – nor has it ever been, despite previous appearances – but of purely mental scrutiny; and this can be imperfect and confused, as it was before, or clear and distinct as it is now, depending on how carefully I concentrate on what the wax consists in. (AT VII 31: CSM II 21)

The main thrust of this passage is that the wax appears to the senses in various, changeable ways, but what the wax really consists in remains the same throughout these sensible changes, and is perceived by the mind alone.

The Meditator is more precise about which mental faculty is at work here. It is the faculty of judgment – the mind judges that, despite those sensible changes, the same wax remains. The role of judgment here is intended to show that the mind is better known than the body:

> Surely my awareness of my own self is not merely much truer and more certain than my awareness of the wax, but also much more distinct and evident. For if I judge that the wax exists from the fact that I see it, clearly this same fact entails much more evidently that I myself also exist. (AT VII 33: CSM II 22)

Presumably his knowledge of himself is 'truer', 'more certain' and more 'distinct and evident' than his knowledge of the wax, because his perception of himself did not change but was stable unlike his sensory perception of the wax. The further claim is made that the Meditator's *judgement* that the wax exists also very clearly entails that 'I myself also exist'. But how? The answer is found in the fact that the wax, or any body for that matter, is perceived by the mind alone. As a result, every perception of a body entails a sensory, imaginative or intellectual act, which, in turn, implies the existence of a thinking thing or mind to perform that activity. So the existence of the mind is proven by each and every perception of a body, while the existence of bodies is still in doubt. Hence knowledge of the mind's existence is both prior to and better than knowledge of bodies.

The mind is also better known in that the Meditator perceives more properties in himself than are perceived in bodies. This is best explained in the following excerpt from *Principles* I.11:

> Now we find more attributes in our mind than in anything else, as is manifest from the fact that whatever enables us to know anything else cannot but lead us to a much surer knowledge of our own mind. (AT VIIIA 8: CSM I 196)

Here Descartes is saying that the mind has an 'attribute' or idea for everything it perceives both internally and externally to itself. For every quality perceived in a body, there is a corresponding perception or thought in the mind. But in addition to these perceptions of bodily qualities, the mind also has perceptions of itself, which are also mental qualities or 'attributes', i.e. thoughts. Accordingly, the mind perceives itself as having 'attributes' derived from the perception of both bodily and mental qualities, whereas it perceives bodies as having only bodily 'attributes'. Therefore, it perceives twice as many qualities in itself as it does in bodies. It is this sheer quantity of perceptions about the mind over those of the body that also make the mind better known than the body.

This effort is supposed to free readers of the *Meditations* from their reliance on sense perception for attaining certain knowledge. Indeed, such reliance could lead people astray into thinking that the hard and cold wax was not the same as the soft and hot wax, because the sensible qualities of the wax have changed. But it is only through the mental operation of judgment, which is just intellect and will working in tandem, that certain knowledge about the persistence of the same wax is attained. Moreover, given how the perceptions of mental qualities outnumber those of physical qualities, things that cannot be seen, heard, touched, tasted or smelled are actually better known than things, like the wax, which are perceivable by sensation. Hence, for Descartes, sensation is not a help but a hindrance in obtaining certain knowledge. Accordingly, it should be cast aside in favour of pure thought.

CHAPTER 3

METAPHYSICS

This chapter takes a look at the roots of Descartes' philosophical tree, i.e. his metaphysics, which can be characterized as a theory of fundamental reality. This chapter's first three sections examine the various categories of things Descartes considers most fundamental, namely substances, modes and attributes. The remaining three sections discuss other areas of both traditional metaphysical concern (i.e. the nature of universals) as well as important metaphysical theses about the degrees of reality and what is necessary for one thing to be the cause of another, which are so important to the causal arguments for God's existence discussed in the next chapter.

3.1 THEORY OF DISTINCTION

Criteria for distinguishing between things of various categories are important tools for figuring out where something fits into a metaphysics. These distinctions are the real distinctions between substances, the modal distinction either between a mode and its underlying substance or between two or more modes of the same substance, and the rational distinction between an essential attribute and its substance or two attributes of one and the same substance. Each of these will be discussed in turn.

Descartes explains the real distinction in the following passage from *Principles* I.60:

> Strictly speaking, a *real* distinction exists only between two or more substances; and we can perceive that two substances are really distinct simply from the fact that we can clearly and distinctly understand one apart from the other. For when we come to know

God, we are certain that he can bring about anything of which we have a distinct understanding. (AT VIIIA 28: CSM I 213)

According to this passage, two things are really distinct substances if each can be clearly and distinctly understood or intellectually perceived 'apart' from the other. Further light is shed on this in a letter of 2 May 1644 to the Jesuit priest and ardent supporter of Descartes, Denis Mesland. Here a distinction is made between abstraction and exclusion:

> There is a great difference between *abstraction* and *exclusion*. If I said simply that the idea which I have of my soul does not represent it to me as being dependent on the body and identified with it, this would be merely an abstraction, from which I could form only a negative argument which would be unsound. But I say that this idea represents it to me as a substance which can exist even though everything belonging to the body be excluded from it; from which I form a positive argument, and conclude that it can exist without the body. (AT IV 120: CSM K 236)

This clear and distinct understanding of one substance apart from another is not the result of abstracting one from the other but is based on the ability to exclude the concept of one from that of another. For example, all that pertains to the mind, e.g. understanding, willing, affirming, denying, etc., is completely excluded from the understanding of body. Likewise all that pertains to body, e.g. shape, size, position and motion, is completely excluded from the understanding of mind. Therefore, the intellectual perceptions of mind alone and body alone are clear and distinct, because whatever pertains to one can be excluded from the other (AT VII 28: CSM II 48; and AT VIIIA 29: CSM I 13).

While exclusion is a kind of organization of concepts into what is perceived to be or not to be a part of this or that concept, abstraction occurs when a part of an idea is considered in isolation from the rest of that idea. So, in the case of a real distinction, the mind is not some part of the idea of body that is being isolated and considered all by itself. Instead, the concept of the mind and that of the body are each being understood as mutually exclusive such that what pertains to one does not pertain to the other without any overlap between them. This mutual exclusivity indicates to Descartes that the two things represented by these concepts are really distinct substances.

However, making the inference from the independence of these two concepts to the independence of the two things represented by them traverses a logical gap from how things are conceived to how they are in reality. For Descartes, this logical gap is bridged by the knowledge of God and the fact that 'he can bring about anything about which we have a distinct understanding'. This speaks directly to the issue of God's power. The point is that the ability to clearly and distinctly perceive something apart from something else and vice versa signifies that God *could* create one without the other if he wished. This means that God could create a world in which that one thing existed all by itself without any other created thing. Thus, a real distinction between two or more substances indicates that it is possible for each of the entities to exist alone without the other, at least by the power of God. This will be important in 3.2 where Descartes' conception of substance is discussed in more detail.

Descartes recognizes two kinds of modal distinction at *Principles* I.61. These are the modal distinctions between a mode and its underlying substance and that of two or more modes of one and the same substance. The first is marked by the fact that all that pertains to one of the entities to be distinguished can be excluded from the other but not vice versa. For example, an extended substance, like a piece of clay, can be understood without being any particular shape such that it could be square, round or triangle-shaped without ceasing to be clay or an extended substance. But no particular shape, like being round, can be understood without some extended thing or substance having that shape. In other words, a non-extended shape is unintelligible. So, being round cannot be clearly understood without the clay or some kind of extension, while the clay can be understood without it being round. For Descartes, this indicates that the roundness that is really in the clay cannot exist without the clay (or at least some extended thing), while the clay or extended substance can exist without having any particular shape.

The second kind of modal distinction occurs in a similar fashion. For example, all that pertains to the clay's shape can be excluded from its size and vice versa. Accordingly, the clay's size and shape can be clearly and distinctly understood without one another. But as just mentioned, all that pertains to the clay, viz. its extension, cannot be excluded from the concept of its shape or from that of its size, and so they cannot be clearly and distinctly understood without the clay. Hence, size and shape are modes of the clay. However, the clay can be understood to the exclusion of any shape or size, and so the clay is a substance.

The third and final kind of distinction is the rational distinction, which also has two subspecies:

> Finally a *rational distinction* is a distinction between a substance and some attribute of that substance without which the substance is unintelligible; alternatively, it is a distinction between two such attributes of a single substance. (AT VIIIA 30: CSM I 214; translation modified)

Notice that the two kinds of rational distinction roughly correspond to the two kinds of modal distinction in that one is the distinction between an attribute and its substance, while the other is between two or more attributes of one and the same substance. For example, a substance cannot be clearly and distinctly understood without the attribute of duration, 'since a substance cannot cease to endure without also ceasing to be, the distinction between substance and its duration is merely a rational one' (AT VIIIA 30: CSM I 214; translation modified). The point is that none of the entities being distinguished can be fully excluded from the other and therefore each depends on the other for its existence. So, in the case of substance and duration, substance cannot exist without existing for some duration of time, nor can something exist for some duration of time without a substance.

The same criterion is used for distinguishing two attributes of the same substance. In this case, substance cannot be clearly understood without the attributes in question nor can those attributes be clearly and distinctly understood without each other. For example, existence is also an attribute of a substance along with duration. But something cannot endure unless it *exists* for some period of time, and something cannot exist without existing for some *duration* of time. Accordingly, the concept of existence cannot be fully excluded from the concept of duration nor can the concept of duration be fully excluded from the concept of existence. The ontological implication is that a substance cannot exist unless it endures, nor can it endure unless it exists.

The rational distinction is perhaps the most difficult to grasp of the three. This is partly because of the abstract nature of the entities being distinguished (viz. attributes) and partly because of its characterization as a *rational* distinction. This name heavily tempts interpreters to take this to mean that this distinction is a product of the human mind instead of a true distinction found in things themselves. However, this interpretation is undermined by Descartes' claim in a letter to an unknown correspondent that it is a 'distinction made by reason *ratiocinatae*' (AT IV 349: CSM K 280). Here Descartes is making use of a common scholastic-Aristotelian distinction between a rational distinction, *ratiocinatae*, and a rational distinction, *ratiocinantis*. Literally, a rational distinction, *ratiocinantis*, is just a distinction of 'reasoning' reason, whereas a rational distinction, *ratiocinatae*, is literally a distinction of 'reasoned' reason. It is clear from the letter to the unknown correspondent that Descartes' rational distinction is one of 'reasoned' reason and not of 'reasoning' reason'. So, what does all this mean?

Well, a distinction of 'reasoning' reason is one produced by the activity of the mind and is not a true distinction discovered in things themselves. For example, in the sentence 'Socrates is Socrates', Socrates can be distinguished between Socrates as subject and Socrates as predicate. But Socrates himself is neither subject nor predicate. The mind just perceives him in one way and then in another. However, a distinction of 'reasoned' reason is not produced by the mind but is discovered in the things that are being 'reasoned about'. So, 'substance' and 'duration' are not two ways of conceiving the same thing as is the case in conceiving Socrates first as a 'subject' and then as a 'predicate', but rather 'substance' and 'duration' are two features (or attributes) found in something, e.g. a ball, and without which that thing cannot exist. Therefore, Descartes' rational distinction is not a mere matter of perspective or mere invention of the mind, but it is a distinction discovered in things themselves as is the case with the real and modal distinctions. The fact that all of these distinctions mark off different metaphysical entities found in things themselves prompts closer looks at Descartes' more considered views of substance, mode and attribute.

3.2 SUBSTANCE AND MODE

Descartes defines the term 'substance' in two different ways. The definition found in the 'Geometrical Exposition' in the *Second Replies* characterizes substance as the subject of properties, while the account found at *Principles* I.51 describes substance as something that requires nothing else for its existence. At first glance, these might appear to be two completely different definitions – indeed, this is the view of many scholars.[1] However, an important point to recognize is that the *Principles* describes substance by means of its *independence* from anything else (with some qualification as will be discussed below), while the *Second Replies* defines substance by means of the *dependence* of various properties on it. A closer look at each of these two accounts will show how they are not so different but are really two sides of the same coin.

Let us begin with the *Second Replies*' 'definition' of substance as the subject in which properties reside.[2]

> *Substance*: This term applies to every thing in which whatever we perceive immediately resides, as in a subject, or to everything by means of which whatever we perceive exists. By 'whatever we perceive' is meant any property, quality or attribute of which we have a real idea. The only idea we have of substance itself, in the strict sense, is that it is the thing in which whatever we perceive (or whatever has objective being in one of our ideas) exists, either formally or eminently. For we know by the natural light that a real attribute cannot belong to nothing. (AT VII 161: CSM II 114)

The first line of this passage indicates substance's role as the subject of 'whatever we immediately perceive', which is described in the next sentence as 'any property, quality or attribute of which we have a real idea.'[3] So these properties, qualities or attributes reside in a substance as in a subject. However, this 'residence' of properties in their substances turns out to be quite a strong relation, for substances are the foundation on which such properties exist. In other words, these properties, qualities or attributes depend on substance for their existence.

Another interesting and important feature of this 'definition' is the claim that people only have the ideas of these perceptible properties and do not, strictly speaking, have the idea of substance. This point is reiterated at *Principles* I.52:

> However, we cannot initially become aware of a substance merely through its being an existing thing, since this alone does not of itself have any effect on us. We can, however, easily come to know a substance by one of its attributes, in virtue of the common notion that nothingness possesses no attributes, that is to say, no properties or qualities. (AT VIIIA 25: CSM I 210)

In both texts Descartes argues that people have only indirect knowledge of substance via the perception of any one of its attributes. Accordingly, the idea people have of substance is a result of a deduction made from the intuition that 'a real attribute cannot belong to nothing.' For example, from the existence of doubting, which is a real attribute or mode, 'I' can deduce the existence of some thing doing the doubting, viz. an 'I' or mind, which is an immaterial substance, because such a 'real attribute' or mode cannot belong to no subject whatsoever. Hence, attributes, like understanding $2 + 2 = 4$, or shapes, cannot exist independently of understanding and shaped things themselves – there is no such thing as an idea floating freely without a mind, or a shape that is not extended. So, a substance is the subject in which a property, quality or attribute must reside in order to exist and there is no direct perception of substance itself. So whatever knowledge of substance people may have is the result of a deduction from the existence of some property to that in which that property must reside in order to exist, viz. a substance.

This brings us to a discussion of 'modes'. It is not evident at first glance that the properties, qualities or attributes of the *Second Replies* also include modes. Light is shed on this issue by Descartes' recognition in *Comments on a Certain Broadsheet* that the term 'attribute' is 'whatever we recognize as being naturally ascribable to something, whether it be a mode which is susceptible of change, or the absolutely immutable essence of the thing in question' (AT VIIIB 348: CSM I 297). Hence, on the one hand, 'attribute' refers to an essential feature of something that is only rationally distinct from substance in the sense discussed above. On the other hand, 'attribute' can also be used to designate changeable features of a thing such as when the wax's shape changes while the wax itself remains in existence. This provides some evidence that the term 'attribute' as used in the *Second Replies* account of substance is referring to naturally ascribable properties that are susceptible to change, i.e. modes.

So then what is a mode and in what sense does it 'reside' in a substance? The English term 'mode' is just a transliteration of the Latin *modus*, which means 'way' or 'manner'. Hence, a mode is just a way or manner of being something. Fundamentally, this must be a way of being a thinking or an extended thing (as discussed below at 3.3). For example, a ball being sphere-shaped is just one of the ways in which that body is extended. Similarly, understanding that $2 + 2 = 4$ is just one of the ways in which the mind thinks. This implies further that modes require a substance in order to exist. This is brought out in Descartes' account of the modal distinction where the inability to fully exclude the concept of extension from the concept of size, for example, is supposed to show that size depends on extension for its existence. Hence, all modes require a substance in which to reside in order to exist. But remember that the first kind of modal distinction shows that although modes depend on substances for their existence, substances do not require any particular mode to exist.

This independence leads directly to Descartes' second account of substance at *Principles* I.51:

> By *substance* we can understand nothing other than a thing which exists in such a way as to depend on no other thing for its existence. And there is only one substance which can be understood to depend on no other thing whatsoever, namely God. In the case of all other substances, we perceive that they can exist only with the help of God's concurrence. (AT VIIIA 24: CSM I 210)

The first sentence of this passage reiterates substance's ontological independence, while the subsequent ones qualify this independence as it pertains to God and creatures. Strictly speaking, only God is a substance, because only he can exist completely independently of anything else whatsoever. But some things other than God are ontologically dependent on God alone and not on any other creature:

> Hence the term 'substance' does not apply *univocally*, as they say in the Schools, to God and to other things; that is, there is no distinctly intelligible meaning of the term, which is common to God and his creatures. (AT VIIIA 24: CSM I 210)

Yet, even though 'substance' is ambiguous between God and creatures, the two meanings must have something in common to warrant the application of the word to both. The key to solving this mystery is found in a closer examination of the sense in which God, who is the ideal substance, requires nothing else to exist. To begin with, God, like all beings, can be considered dependent on the attributes internal to his essence or nature. For example, if an essential attribute of a (Euclidean) triangle is to have three sides, then the existence of triangle xyz depends on the fact that it has three sides. If it gains or loses a side, then triangle xyz ceases to exist because it is no longer a triangle. God also has an essence, which is composed of a set of essential attributes like omnipotence, omniscience, supreme perfection, etc. Now, surely if the being called 'God' lacked any one of these attributes, he would no longer be God but some less perfect being. Therefore, even God depends on his own essence in order to exist. But notice that only God 'depends on no *other* thing whatsoever', and hence God's status as a substance rests upon his independence from everything else *besides* himself. Therefore, God is absolutely independent of anything else.

Now, since everything else is a creation of God and, therefore, depends on God for its existence, nothing else besides God is a substance strictly speaking. However, those creatures that require *only* God to exist are also substances in a qualified sense. But this raises another perplexing issue: aren't all creatures in some way dependent on other creatures in order to exist? After all, it seems that trees depend on soil, water and sunlight for their existence; and animals depend on water, food, etc. for their existence as well. The sense in which created substances require only God's concurrence can be cleared up by returning to the real distinction wherein two entities are recognized as substances by the mind's ability to clearly and distinctly understand one 'apart' from the other. Recall that this is marked by the ability to fully exclude one perception from the other and vice versa. When this full exclusion occurs, the entity in question is then being clearly and distinctly understood all by itself. This means that God *could* create that thing all by itself, apart from anything else if he so chose.

These considerations provide a solution to the apparent conflict between a creature's dependence on something else and its status as a substance requiring only God to exist. For example, trees actually depend on water, soil and sunlight for their existence. But since God is all powerful, it is *possible* for him to create and sustain that tree in a world with no water, soil or sunlight. Hence, the ability to understand one thing existing all by itself to the exclusion of any other creature signifies people's limited understanding of God's power. In the case of created substance, it means that we know God has the power to create that thing all by itself without any other creature. But when something cannot be clearly and distinctly understood all by itself, such as a cube all by itself without extension, then we do not know whether or not God has the power to create it by itself. Accordingly, something is a created substance only if we know that it *can* exist all by itself depending only on God's power to create and sustain it.

The two accounts of substance examined in this section can now be brought together and harmonized into one, coherent account. Each can be summed up as follows:

1. The subject in which modes reside,
2. Something requiring only God's creative and sustaining power to exist.

Notice that in (1) substance is defined by a mode's ontological dependence on it, whereas in (2) substance is accounted for by its ontological independence of everything but God. Taken together, these two features indicate substance's role as the ultimate substratum in which resides all that is perceived. This substratum is 'ultimate' in that created substances do not reside in anything else but are the substrata in which all modes must reside in order to exist. The importance of such an entity in Descartes' metaphysics is to stave off an infinite regress of modes. For, according to Descartes, a mode does not need to reside directly in some substance but can reside in another mode (see the letter of April 1641 to the famous English philosopher, Thomas Hobbes, AT III 355–6: CSM K 178). However, it would be unintelligible for this residence of one mode in another to go on for ever – it must stop somewhere. Something that does not reside in anything else is needed in order to stop this infinite regress of modes. Substance's ontological independence fills this role. Therefore, a created substance is just something that does not reside in anything else, and as a result constitutes the basic metaphysical ground for the rest of created reality.

Unpacking created substance's independent existence by means of its non-residence in some other creature is confirmed in the following excerpt from the French edition of *Principles* I.51:

> In the case of created things, some are of such a nature that they cannot exist without other things, while some need only the ordinary concurrence of God in order to exist. We make this distinction by calling the latter 'substances' and the former 'qualities' or 'attributes' of those substances. (AT VIIIA 24: CSM I 210)

Notice that in this passage Descartes contrasts the independent existence of substances with the dependent existence of 'qualities' or 'attributes', which are presumably what he would later call a 'mode' in a strict sense. The point is that substances do not have an existence that is dependent on other things in the same way as modes.

Accordingly, substances do not reside in some other creature as do modes.

The situation is different for God, because he does not have any modes but only attributes, 'since in the case of God, any variation is unintelligible' (*Principles* I.56, AT VIIIA 26: CSM I 211). Accordingly, God's status as a substance is not a result of not residing in some other thing and being an ultimate subject of modes, but rather on being the ultimate source of existence. This also means that created substances have a different sort of dependence on God than modes have on created substance. Created substances (and their modes) do not reside in God as modes in a substance, since God cannot have any modes. But all creatures depend on God for their existence, because he is the creative cause that not only brings everything else into existence but also sustains or conserves their existence from moment to moment. Therefore, created substances depend on God as the cause of their sustained existence, and as such God's creations are separate from him.

3.3 ATTRIBUTES

Having discussed the objects of the real and modal distinctions, it is now time to turn to the object of the rational distinction, viz. attributes. Descartes specifically addresses attributes in the following excerpt from *Principles* I.56:

> [F]inally, when we are simply thinking in a more general way of what is in a substance, we use the term *attribute*. Hence we do not, strictly speaking, say that there are modes or qualities in God, but simply attributes, since in the case of God, any variation is unintelligible. And even in the case of created things, that which always remains unmodified – for example existence or duration in a thing which exists and endures – should be called not a quality or mode but an attribute. (AT VIIIA 26: CSM I 211–12)

Contrary to modes, which are changeable ways of being something, attributes are unchangeable properties of things. Recall further that a substance can continue to exist despite a change in any one of its modes, but a substance will cease to exist without any one of its attributes. This indicates that attributes are internal to the essence or nature of a substance, while modes are external to that essence or nature. At this point, it will be convenient to make a further distinction between general attributes and the principal attributes.[4]

Some of the most general attributes of things are substance, duration, order and number (see *Principles* I.48, AT VIIIA 22–3: CSM I 208), which pertain to 'all classes of things'. This means that these attributes must in some way be present in anything in order for it to exist, and as such each is only rationally distinct from substance and from each other. However, all things can be broken down into two principal classes of things, namely thinking and extension. Perception and will are attributed to thinking, while size, shape, motion, position and divisibility are attributed to extension. Notice that shape, for example, cannot be referred to thinking, nor can perception or will be referred to extension. This means that ultimately each substance is either thinking or extended, and that only certain kinds of modes can reside in a thinking substance while another kind of mode can reside only in an extended substance.

But it is also important to notice that these principal attributes denote the 'ultimate classes of things'. This does not preclude the possibility of there being a non-ultimate kind of thing that is in some sense both thinking and extended. Descartes makes reference to such things near the end of *Principles* I.48:

> But we also experience within ourselves certain other things which must not be referred either to the mind alone or to the body alone. These arise . . . from the close and intimate union of our mind with the body. (AT VIIIA 23: CSM I 209)

According to this passage, some things cannot be referred to the mind or the body individually but are the result of their union. This is an important issue to be discussed in Chapter 7. But for now the important point is that some modes, such as appetites like hunger and thirst, emotions, such as anger, joy, sadness and love as well as sensations, such as pain, pleasure, light, sounds, smells, tastes, etc. are not to be referred to the mind or body alone but the entity that results from their union. This union would then be an essential attribute of the composite mind and body, i.e. human being, since without it the composite would cease to exist. But union is not a principal attribute since it does not constitute an ultimate class of things.

3.4 ABSTRACTION AND UNIVERSALS

The problem of universals had been a hot topic among philosophers for centuries before Descartes. This problem stems largely from a problem of word reference. Universal or general words like 'man', 'animal', 'plant', 'horse', 'number', etc. are used when talking about particular things such as this man named 'John' or this dog named 'Rover'. It was commonly assumed that all words, including universal or general terms, derive their meaning by referring to something. However, although universal or general terms might be used to describe this or that particular thing, e.g. 'Rover is a dog' where the word 'dog' is being used to describe something about Rover, it cannot get its entire meaning from its reference to Rover. If this were the case, then Rover would be the only dog in existence, but this is surely not true. So it was often thought that universal words like 'dog' must refer to something besides this or that particular dog so that the word can be used meaningfully with regards to any number of particular dogs.

Although a vast array of theories about universals arose over the centuries, three fundamental theories were most prevalent. The first is Platonism. This theory is based on Plato's theory of Forms or Ideas, which were thought to exist in a realm that was not accessible to any of the five senses but to the mind alone. These Forms or Ideas were just the definitions, essences or natures of dogness itself, human being itself, piety itself, triangle itself, etc. So, on this account, universal terms have meaning because they refer to these Forms or Ideas; and particular things exemplify those Forms or Ideas to some extent or other such that the word 'dog' was thought to be truthfully asserted of something only if it exemplified dogness itself. Christian philosophers eventually took these Platonic ideas and placed them in the mind of God such that contemplation of these various natures constituted a kind of intellectual communion with the Divine essence.

Another theory is known as 'nominalism'. This theory states that universals are mere words without any real reference. Here the key term is 'real'. Nominalists believed that universal terms referred to collections of things with certain properties in common. However, these collections themselves were not the actual collections of things existing in the world. That is, words like 'dog' do not refer to the collection of actual dogs existing in the world, but rather this collection was considered to be a logical entity. These logical collections were then defined by some common set of properties such that anything existing in the past, present or future or even not at all (like a unicorn) would be a member of a given collection. So, for the nominalist, universal words derive their meaning by referring to these logical collections.

At this point the reader may have noticed that Platonism claims that universals are robustly real – indeed, according to Plato, Forms or Ideas are most real while the world of particular, changing things is not so real. But universals have a very weak reality for the nominalist; it is just a matter of words and logic. A middle ground can be found in what is nowadays called 'conceptualism'. This theory grounds the reality of universals in particular things themselves, like this man named 'John' or this dog named 'Rover', but fixes their reference to concepts or ideas in the human mind. The gist is that human beings get universal or general ideas from experiences of particular things. For example, people experience many different animals and then notice that some of them have certain features in common. These features are then abstracted from these experiences to form the universal or general idea of a dog, for example. The process of abstraction, however, varies among philosophers as well, and this gives rise to various forms of 'conceptualism'. Descartes falls into this conceptualist camp with his own theory of abstraction.

It is apparent from 3.1 that Descartes' doctrine of distinction rests squarely on the ability or inability to fully exclude one perception, concept or idea from another. But just because something cannot be fully excluded from something else does not mean that it cannot be abstracted. For example, the idea of a stone's shape cannot be fully excluded from the idea of the stone itself, since that shape is one of the stone's modes. However, the stone's shape can still be considered in isolation from the rest of the idea of the stone itself. It is this isolation of one aspect of a complete idea that Descartes calls 'abstraction', and it is by means of this process that the universal or general ideas, such as the idea of shape in general, come into existence.

Descartes makes this point about the ideas of order, duration and number at *Principles* I. 55:

> We shall also have a very distinct understanding of *duration, order* and *number*, provided we do not mistakenly tack on to them any concept of substance. Instead, we should regard the duration of a thing simply as a mode under which we conceive the thing in so far as it continues to exist. And similarly we should not regard order or number as anything separate from the things which are

ordered and numbered, but should think of them simply as modes under which we consider the things in question. (AT VIIIA 26: CSM I 211)

This is a complicated passage that requires some close attention. First, Descartes exhorts his reader not to 'tack on' a concept of substance to his understanding of duration, order and number. The warning is to avoid understanding these attributes as things that can exist all by themselves. Although this may seem strange to the twenty-first-century reader, Descartes is here rejecting the Platonic notion of universals where universals were thought to exist all by themselves in a non-sensible but intelligible realm of their own.

Second, later in this passage, Descartes claims that order and number are found only in ordered and numbered things. Further light is shed on this at *Principles* I.58:

In the same way, number, when it is considered simply in the abstract or in general, and not in any created thing, is merely a mode of thinking; and the same applies to all other *universals*, as we call them. (AT VIIIA 27: CSM I 212)

Here Descartes is explicit that the general idea of number is an abstraction from numbered things and in this way universals are ideas in the mind, under which 'we consider the things in question'.[5] For example, in the sentence 'The stone is round', the stone is being considered under the idea of shape; in the sentence 'The stone is heavy', the stone is being considered under the idea of heaviness or weight, and so on. So, for Descartes, universals exist only as ideas in the mind and universal or general words have meaning only because they refer to these abstracted ideas.

3.5 DEGREES OF REALITY

Substances and modes also admit various degrees and kinds of reality. It has already been mentioned that thinking and extension are the principal attributes constituting the fundamental kinds of things existing in the universe. But these two basic kinds of reality also admit of degrees: all thinking things are either finite or infinite and all extended things are either finite or indefinite. A finite thing is just something with limits. In both Part IV of the *Discourse* and the *Third Meditation*, the fact that 'I' am finite is deduced from that fact that 'I' am doubting, 'for I saw clearly that it is a greater perfection to know than to doubt' (AT VI 33: CSM I 127–8). Hence, doubting is a less perfect state than knowledge, and so the 'I' or any mind is limited in this way. But the idea of God is that of an infinite thinking substance. For instance, God is all-knowing, and so there is nothing he does not know or anything that he can call into doubt. God also has many other infinite attributes that created minds have in a limited way, such as power, goodness, etc. Indeed, for Descartes knowledge of the infinite substance called 'God' is prior to knowledge of the 'I' as finite:

> For how could I understand that I doubted or desired – that is, lacked something – and that I was not wholly perfect, unless there were in me some idea of a more perfect being which enabled me to recognize my own defects by comparison? (AT VII 45–6: CSM II 31)

In this passage from the *Third Meditation*, the prior idea of an infinite being is necessary for the Meditator to discover his own finitude. This is because he had to compare himself to some standard in order to realize that he had limits to his knowledge, power, etc. All of this implies that 'I' lack some perfections, while God lacks no perfections or is absolutely perfect. Accordingly, the infinite is not a negation of the finite, as the word itself might suggest, but rather the finite is the negation of the infinite, because 'infinite' denotes absolute perfection, while 'finite' denotes some kind of imperfection.

It is important here to acknowledge that Descartes uses the term 'infinite' in a slightly different way than its common usage. In common parlance, 'infinite' is often used to mean something like 'it goes on for ever'. The usual example is that numbers go on and on without end. But for Descartes, 'infinite' should be reserved for God alone, '[f]or in the case of God alone, not only do we fail to recognize any limits in any respect, but our understanding positively tells us that there are none' (AT VIIIA 15: CSM I 202). So, in the case of God, it is not an understanding of what is *not* recognized about something, viz. a limit, but rather the recognition that God actually does not have any limits. The point is more clearly made when Descartes contrasts the infinite with the indefinite at *Principles* I.27:

> Secondly, in the case of other things, our understanding does not in the same way positively tell us that they lack limits in some respect; we merely acknowledge in a negative way that any limits

which they may have cannot be discovered by us. (AT VIIIA 15: CSM I 202)

Here Descartes makes it clear that people merely recognize their inability to discover a limit, which leaves open the possibility of there being a limit beyond the finite powers of human perception. This is what Descartes calls the 'indefinite' and is applied to the physical universe. For example, 'no matter how great we imagine the number of stars to be, we still think that God could have created even more; and so we will suppose the number of stars to be indefinite' (AT VIIIA 15: CSM I 202). However, particular extended things, like this tree or that stone, are presumably finite, because they have limiting surfaces, i.e. they have a discoverable limit.

This taxonomy indicates a gradation of reality from most real or perfect down to what is least real or perfect. Recall that God, who is an infinite substance, is absolutely perfect, while created things are finite or, at best, indefinite. This implies that an infinite substance is more perfect than a finite substance. In other words, God has more perfections than any finite substance because he actually has all perfections, whereas finite substances actually have some, potentially have others, but they never actually have all of them. In this way, God can be said to be more real than any finite thing, and therefore he is the most real of anything. God's infinitude and absolute perfection also means that he has the perfection of actual existence (see 4.4). This then implies that God does not depend on anything else besides his own perfection in order to exist. Hence, God is at the top of the chain because he requires absolutely nothing else in order to exist. Recall further that some creatures are substances in a qualified sense of the term in that they rely on nothing but God for their existence, and therefore created substances are second most real. But recall too that modes also require a created substance in which to reside in order to exist. Accordingly, modes require both God and a created substance in order to exist, and so modes are least real. Hence, the degrees of reality can be listed from most to least real as follows:

1. Infinite Substance
2. Finite Substance
3. Mode

This ranking will be particularly important for understanding

Descartes' primary causal argument for the existence of God discussed in the next chapter.

3.6 THE CAUSAL ADEQUACY PRINCIPLE

Another important feature of Descartes' metaphysics is the principle by which substances and modes can causally interact. This causal principle determines what sort of thing, be it substance, mode or idea, can cause the existence of something else. As might be expected, the answer to the question of 'what can cause what?' is based on the degrees of reality discussed in the previous section. Descartes answers this question by proposing a principle for determining what is required for something to be the adequate cause of something else.

Descartes lays out his causal principle in the *Third Meditation* as follows: 'Now it is manifest by the natural light that there must be at least as much reality in the efficient and total cause as in the effect of that cause' (AT VII 40: CSM II 28). The reality of some effect must receive that reality from a cause that itself possesses that reality. As a result, something with less reality cannot cause something with more reality, '[f]or where, I ask, could the effect get its reality from, if not from the cause? And how could the cause give it to the effect unless it possessed it?' (AT VII 40: CSM II 28)

This couplet of rhetorical questions expresses a 'giving and receiving' conception of causation. Though this is not the place for a thorough discussion of Descartes' theory of causation, suffice it to say that whatever reality an effect has was given to it by a cause that already had it. An example of an ordinary case of giving and receiving should prove helpful here. Suppose a friend gives you a book for your birthday. Now, your friend cannot give you the book unless she has bought it or come to possess it in some way, for if she were to give you a book she does not have, then she would be giving you nothing. Hence, a necessary condition for your having the reality of possessing that book is that the cause of your possessing it must herself have had the reality of possessing that book. This is basically how Descartes understands the cause-effect relation. He provides his own illustration a few lines later:

A stone, for example, which previously did not exist, cannot begin to exist unless it is produced by something which contains, either formally or eminently everything to be found in the stone; similarly, heat cannot be produced in an object which was not previously hot, except by something of at least the same order of perfection as heat, and so on. (AT VII 41: CSM II 28)

At first glance, the latter case seems to say that a pot of cold water, for instance, can only be brought to a boil by some cause (e.g. a flame) that is at least that hot, because only something at 100°C or more can give that much heat to the pot of cold water. This interpretation is a little misleading, because the Meditator does not exactly say this but only that the heat must be caused by something of the same 'order' (or 'degree' or 'kind', added in the French edition), which raises a question about the meaning of the term 'order' here. Does it mean that only heat can beget heat and motion can beget motion? Or, does it mean that only something of the same order, degree or kind of *reality* can cause it? The answers to these questions will be provided in Chapter 7 when the problem of mind-body causal interaction is discussed. But this interpretation of the heat example will do for now, since it nicely illustrates the giving and receiving model of causality at the root of Descartes' causal principle.

The stone example, however, packs in yet another metaphysical distinction, namely the distinction between formal and eminent reality. 'Formal' reality stems from the scholastic conception of a form, which was the principle by which the potential for a reality is actualized. Returning to the heat example, the cold water in the pot has the potential to boil regardless of whether or not it has a sufficient heat source. But it is that source, e.g. a flame, that has the form of heat and turns the cold water from potentially boiling to actually boiling. Hence, something has a reality formally when it actually has that reality. So, in the case of a stone, an actual stone can cause the existence of another stone. Eminent reality is a little trickier. A reality is possessed eminently when that reality is not possessed formally but in a higher form such that it has more than enough reality to produce it formally in some effect. For instance, God is believed to be the creator, i.e. the efficient and total cause, of the entire physical universe. Yet God is not a physical or material entity but an infinite thinking substance. Accordingly, God is not formally a material thing but he has the power to produce material things such as stones, plants and the entire physical universe, since he is an infinite substance and these things are merely finite or indefinite. So, although God is not formally extended, he has extension eminently.

Another important feature of Descartes' causal principle within the context of the *Meditations* is that the Meditator claims to know it 'by the natural light' thereby indicating that it is known by intuition, i.e. in one, sweeping mental glance, and so it is supposed to be beyond doubt in the same way as 'I think, therefore I am' is beyond doubt. From his examination of this intuition, the Meditator is able to make two further deductions:

> It follows from this both that something cannot arise from nothing, and also that what is more perfect – that is, contains in itself more reality – cannot arise from what is less perfect. (AT VII 40–1: CSM II 28)

It is easy to see how this follows from the giving and receiving model of causation. The first inference that 'something cannot arise from nothing' is really just a different way of stating the original causal principle in that nothing literally has nothing to give to anything else. The second inference further restates the original principle but in terms of the degrees of reality. For something cannot give to something (or cause it to have) a reality or perfection that it does not itself possess, e.g. your friend gives you nothing, if she tries to give you a book she doesn't have. Accordingly, these further truths are both deductions from the original principle, and they are also intuitions since the entire deductive chain is short enough to be grasped in a single mental glance. Now, it is important to apply the causal principle to the degrees of reality in order to show what can cause what:

Cause	Effect
Infinite Substance	Finite Substance, or Mode
Finite Substance	Finite Substance, or Mode
Mode	Mode

However, this principle does not just apply to substances and modes themselves but also to the ideas the Meditator has of them. Ideas themselves are just modes of a thinking substance and, to that extent, it would be possible for the Meditator, a finite substance, to be the cause of all his ideas. But the objective reality any idea contains is another story. Recall from 2.4 that an idea's objective reality is a representation of some thing and exists in the mind in the way things normally exist there. Accordingly, an idea of a chair, for instance, contains that chair not formally (which would be absurd) but objectively. The Meditator argues that the causal principle applies to the causes of the objective reality contained in ideas, because these realities, though in some sense less real than formally existing things like chairs, are still something and, therefore, they could not have come from nothing; that is, they also require an adequate cause. Hence, any idea must receive its objective reality 'from some cause which contains at least as much formal reality as there is objective reality in the idea' (AT VII 41: CSM II 28; see also *Principles* I.17, AT VIIIA 11: CSM I 198). So, based on this principle, the mind can be the adequate cause of an idea of a finite substance, because it is itself a finite substance. It can also cause the idea of some mode since it is real to a higher degree, i.e. it is eminently a mode. One can quickly see where the Meditator is going with this: the idea of an infinite substance, i.e. a supremely perfect being, cannot be caused by a finite substance but only by something that is formally an infinite substance, i.e. God himself (see *Principles* I.18, AT VIIIA 11–12: CSM I 199). How this principle and the degrees of reality play out in the causal arguments for God's existence will be addressed in the next chapter.

CHAPTER 4

RELIGION

The existence of God is particularly important to Descartes' overall philosophical project because it is one of two metaphysical theses that provide his absolutely certain foundation for knowledge, which secures the rest of the philosophical tree. Accordingly, most of this chapter is devoted to expositions and analyses of Descartes' arguments for the existence of God. However, other aspects of his religious thought are also addressed, including the immortality of the soul and the miracle of the Eucharist. But first a brief look at Descartes' views on the role of reason in religious matters is in order.

4.1 FAITH AND REASON

The tension between faith and reason was an issue of much debate among the learned of Descartes' time. The hotness of this debate was largely due to differences in religious doctrine between the various Protestant denominations and the Catholic Church. The tension stems from the fact that beliefs based on reason have arguments and evidence to support them, while beliefs based on faith do not. This is, of course, not to say that faith is irrational, or contrary to reason, but only that it is non-rational. But what if a rational belief comes into conflict with, or maybe even contradicts, a belief based on faith? For example, the law of non-contradiction is a basic rational principle stating that anything implying a contradiction cannot be true. But the Incarnation (i.e. the claim that God became human in Christ) seems to imply a contradiction, for how can an infinite being like God also be a finite human being? This would mean that the same being is both finite and infinite at the same time, which is contradictory. Thus this fundamental doctrine of Christian faith seems to violate a basic law of reason.

There are many ways to approach this problem. One is to deny any conflict by maintaining that all articles of faith are at least not irrational and can even be supported by reason if one searched hard enough. This would be a very optimistic view of reason as applied to doctrines of religious faith, for it maintains that rational arguments could be provided for even the seemingly contradictory doctrines such as the Incarnation. Another approach is to give precedence to one or the other so that faith would trump reason or vice versa. On this account, someone committed to reason would have to reject any doctrine of faith that could not be supported by rational grounds, whereas someone committed to faith would reject any dictate of reason that conflicted with an article of faith. Yet another way of dealing with this difficulty is to mark off faith and reason into two different domains of knowledge so that neither can trespass into the other's territory. This would mean that reason should not be used to justify religious doctrine nor should religious doctrine be used to trump any conclusion reached by reason.

Given his commitment to the geometrical method discussed in Chapter 1, it might seem that Descartes would be entirely committed to the first approach where reason extends even to apparently contradictory articles of faith like the Incarnation. However, he takes a much more moderate approach that is somewhat in line with the last option. Descartes believes that there are some doctrines of the Church, like the Incarnation and the Trinitarian God, that are beyond the limits of human reason, and they should, therefore, be accepted on faith. But there are other religious truths that can be reached through reason. In fact, some are better reached in this way for the sake of converting non-believers:

> I have always thought that two topics – namely God and the soul – are prime examples of subjects where demonstrative proofs ought to be given with the aid of philosophy rather than theology. For us who are believers, it is enough to accept on faith that the human soul does not die with the body, and that God exists; but in the case of unbelievers, it seems that there is no religion, and practically no moral virtue, that they can be persuaded to adopt until these two truths are proved to them by natural reason. (AT VII 1–2: CSM II 3)

In this excerpt from the Dedicatory Letter to the Faculty at the Sorbonne prefacing the *Meditations*, Descartes makes two important points. The first is that questions concerning the existence of God and the immortality of the soul can be answered by way of rational demonstration and, therefore, these doctrines do not need to be accepted on faith alone. Second, non-believers need to be persuaded of these truths by reason. In this way, reason serves religious faith as a tool of conversion. A few paragraphs later, Descartes picks out those who maintain by reason that the soul dies with the body but hold the opposite view by faith alone. He then invokes the command of the Lateran Council under Pope Leo X that 'condemned those who take this position, and expressly enjoined Christian philosophers to refute their arguments and use all their powers to establish the truth' (AT VII 3: CSM II 4). Descartes claims to take up this challenge in his attempts to demonstrate the real distinction between mind and body and God's existence. Many scholars believe that Descartes is being insincere about his role as a Defender of the Faith. But Descartes is quite vehement in his commitment to the faith in a letter of 25 November 1630 to his frequent correspondent and connection with the intellectual world, Fr Marin Mersenne. There he says that 'I am enraged when I see that there are people in the world so bold and so impudent as to fight against God' (AT I 182: CSMK 29).

Yet, despite this somewhat optimistic role of reason in demonstrating certain doctrines of faith, Descartes is also quick to point out the limits of reason as expressed at *Principles* I.25:

> Hence, if God happens to reveal to us something about himself or others which is beyond the natural reach of our mind – such as the mystery of the Incarnation or of the Trinity – we will not refuse to believe it, despite the fact that we do not clearly understand it. And we will not be at all surprised that there is much, both in the immeasurable nature of God and in the things created by him, which is beyond our mental capacity. (AT VIIIA 14: CSM I 201)

According to this passage, the mysteries of the Christian faith, such as the Incarnation and the Trinity, are not understood as being in conflict with the dictates of reason but as being beyond the capability of reason to understand. So, for Descartes, human reason can penetrate the doctrines of faith – but only so far. Since these mysteries lie beyond the bounds of reason, any conflict they might have with its dictates can legitimately be ignored. However, Descartes is sure to point out in the final section of the *Principles*' first part that beliefs based on the faith in divine revelation trump reason in the few cases where the two might come into conflict:

> But above all else we must impress on our memory the overriding rule that whatever God has revealed to us must be accepted as more certain than anything else. And although the light of reason may, with the utmost clarity and evidence, appear to suggest something different, we must still put our entire faith in divine authority rather than in our own judgement. (AT VIIIA 39: CSM I 221)

So, although Descartes gives reason a wide berth with regard to certain religious issues, he is still obligated to limiting its scope with regard to the mysteries of the faith. The remainder of this chapter examines those religious questions best answered by reason, viz. the existence of God and the immortality of the soul, with a brief look at his reluctant account of one of the Christian mysteries, viz. the miracle of the Eucharist at the end.

4.2 THE CAUSAL ARGUMENTS FOR GOD'S EXISTENCE

The question as to whether or not something besides the Meditator exists arises in the *Third Meditation*. In answering this question, the Meditator is led into a series of three different causal arguments for God's existence, which begins with an enumeration of the various kinds of objective realities he finds in his ideas:

> Among my ideas, apart from the idea which gives me a representation of myself, which cannot present any difficulty in this context, there are ideas which variously represent God, corporeal and inanimate things, angels, animals and finally other men like myself. (AT VII 42–3: CSM II 29)

The Meditator proceeds to examine each of these kinds of ideas to see if any one of them has so much reality that he cannot be the cause of it. The idea of himself is not problematic, since, according to the causal adequacy principle, a finite mind can cause the idea of a finite mind. But what about the rest? Although the Meditator spends some time evaluating them, it is quite evident from what has been said that he could be the cause of his ideas of corporeal things, angels, animals and other men since these are all ideas of other finite substances or modes. Hence, the only possibility remaining is the idea of

God. Since this idea contains the objective reality of an infinite substance, it is impossible for a finite substance like the Meditator to have caused it. Yet it could not have come from nothing; therefore, it must have been caused by something that is formally or actually an infinite substance, i.e. God. Hence, God must exist in order for the Meditator to have this idea of an infinite substance.[1]

The Meditator then raises the following concern about this argument:

> If one concentrates carefully, all this is quite evident by the natural light. But when I relax my concentration, and my mental vision is blinded by the images of things perceived by the senses, it is not so easy for me to remember why the idea of a being more perfect than myself must necessarily proceed from some being which is in reality more perfect. (AT VII 47–8: CSM II 32–3)

Given the level of intricacy and the amount of ground covered in this first causal argument, it is safe to say that this reference to the natural light indicates the Meditator's intuition of each of the deductive steps in the argument. But the clarity and certainty of each step slips away when he lets his guard down and allows images of things to 'blind' him. These images then hinder his already feeble ability to remember how he arrived at this conclusion. These concerns hark back to both Descartes' concerns about the shortcomings of memory discussed in 1.5 and the Meditator's claim about how reliance on the senses obscures the fact that immaterial, thinking things are actually better known than bodies discussed in 2.6. Hence, at the end of the first causal argument, the Meditator is concerned about how the evident nature of this demonstration seems to disappear when the mind's attention is turned away from an immediate intuition of each and every deductive step.

As a result of these concerns, the Meditator decides that he 'should therefore like to go further and inquire whether I myself, who has this idea, could exist if no such being existed' (AT VII 48: CSM II 33). This marks a twofold shift in the Mediator's reasoning. First, he is moving on to consider further causal arguments for the existence of God. Second, these new arguments will not begin merely with the fact that he has the idea of an infinite substance, but they will begin with his own existence as a finite substance with the idea of God. The second argument will focus on an explanation of how he, who is a finite thinking substance with the idea of God, could have come into existence in the first place. The third will focus on explaining why he continues to exist from moment to moment. Each will be discussed in turn.

The second argument is cosmological in nature and begins typically with an attempt to explain the existence of something that is already known. In this case, the Meditator is looking to explain his own existence as a finite thinking substance with the idea of God. Again, the Meditator begins with an enumeration of the possible sources of his existence: 'from myself presumably, or from my parents, or from other beings less perfect than God.' The possibility of the Meditator causing his own existence is ruled out by the fact that he is imperfect, for 'I should neither doubt nor want, nor lack anything at all; for I should have given myself all the perfections of which I have any idea, and thus I should myself be God' (AT VII 48: CSM II 33). Accordingly, if the Meditator were the source of his own existence, then he would not be a finite but an infinite substance. This then contradicts the earlier conclusion that 'I' am finite. Hence, it is impossible for the Meditator himself to be the source of his own existence.

The next option to be scrutinized is whether some other finite substance, such as his parents, could be the cause of his existence. The causal principle makes it evident that a finite substance can cause the existence of another finite substance. The case at hand is just that: his parents are also finite thinking substances with an idea of God, and therefore they could be the cause of another finite thinking substance with an idea of God, viz. the Meditator. This raises the further question: do the Meditator's parents derive their existence from themselves or from some other source? Yet the same considerations that ruled out the Meditator as the source of his own existence also rule out this possibility for his parents. This means that they also derive their existence from something else. Surely the Meditator's parents' parents (i.e. the Meditator's grandparents) could be the cause of their existence as finite thinking substances with an idea of God. But the same question can be raised again about whether their existence is derived from themselves or from another with the same result – they cannot be the source of their own existence and must derive their existence from something else.

The repetition of the same question with the same answer can go on for ever in what is known as an 'infinite regress'. This means that the causal explanation of the existence of finite thinking substances with an idea of God would never be completed, which is commonly considered unintelligible and, therefore, undesirable. From this perspective, something must exist that stops the regress thereby completing the causal explanation. What is required is a being that can explain both its own existence and the existence of finite thinking substances with the idea of God. This being, according to the causal principle, must have either formally or eminently all the reality contained in a finite thinking substance with an idea containing the objective reality of God. Since God is formally or actually an infinite substance, he is also eminently a finite substance. As such, God is both the source of his own existence and can cause the existence of a finite thinking substance with the idea of an infinite substance. Therefore, God must exist, because he is the only possible being that can stop the infinite regress.

What is here being interpreted as a third causal argument is often not considered a stand-alone argument, because it is embedded in the cosmological argument just discussed. It is actually raised as a response to a possible way around the rejection of the Meditator himself as the cause of his own existence:

> I do not escape the force of these arguments by supposing that I have always existed as I do now, as if it followed from this that there was no need to look for any author of my existence. For a lifespan can be divided into countless parts, each completely independent of the others, so that it does not follow from the fact that I existed a little while ago that I must exist now, unless there is some cause which as it were creates me afresh at this moment – that is, which preserves me. (AT VII 48–9: CSM II 33)

Here the Meditator is considering the seeming possibility that there is no cause for his existence, and that he always existed as he is now. The response is that even if this were the case, there would still have to be something that explains his continued existence from moment to moment. Notice that the argument's starting point is not merely the fact that 'I' exist but the fact that 'I' continue to exist over a period of time. This is enough to classify it as a separate argument despite its presentation as a reply to a possible objection to the cosmological argument. This interpretation is also confirmed in the *Principles* where the argument receives independent treatment in Part I, section 21.

Now, the main thrust of this argument is that the Meditator does not intuit any kind of necessary connection between his existing at one moment and his existing at the next. Accordingly, the fact that 'I' am existing now cannot be deduced from the fact that 'I' existed a moment ago. Hence, something must preserve him from moment to moment. This raises the same question as before: can 'I' be the cause of 'my' own preservation from moment to moment or must it be something else? The Meditator's characterization of preservation as re-creation at every moment, albeit metaphorical (as indicated by his use of 'as it were' or *quasi*), already suggests a response. Just as he does not have the power to create himself so also he does not have the power to sustain himself in existence, for 'if there were such a power in me, I should undoubtedly be aware of it. But I experience no such power, and this very fact makes me recognize most clearly that I depend on some being distinct from myself' (AT VII 49: CSM II 34).

Whether this 'being distinct from myself' is another finite substance or an infinite substance is left open at this point. Indeed, the Meditator then proceeds to examine the former option as discussed above. But this argument is a short step away from reaching the conclusion that God exists on its own. For the Meditator's inability to sustain his own existence stems from his status as a finite substance, i.e. his lacking some power. As a result, no finite substance has the power to preserve itself, and therefore some being more perfect, i.e. with more power, is necessary. This being must be an infinite substance, because only an infinite being has the power to sustain both itself and everything else in existence. Therefore, God must exist as the only being capable of preserving the Meditator's existence from moment to moment.

In sum, all three of these arguments rest squarely on the causal adequacy principle and the claim that some things are more or less real than others such that God's existence is deduced from the existence of the idea of God, a finite substance with the idea of God, or the continued existence of such a substance. The main point, then, is that only a formally existing infinite substance can be the cause of the creation and sustained existence of the idea of God itself and the finite thinking substance such a mental mode requires to exist. By the end of the *Third Meditation*, it is no longer a question of what caused the Meditator to have the idea of God, but how it is that God produces this idea in him. It cannot be adventitious because he did not come upon it unexpectedly, and it cannot be fabricated because he cannot add anything to it or subtract anything from it. Therefore, the only remaining option is that the idea of God is innate. Indeed, God placed the idea in him as 'the mark of the craftsman stamped on his work' (AT VII 51: CSM II 35).

4.3 OBJECTIONS TO THE CAUSAL ARGUMENTS

Most people from Descartes' time to the present do not find this series of arguments very convincing, because it rests on the claim that the existence of the idea of God implies the existence of God himself. The gut reaction of most is that just because someone has the idea of something, like Santa Claus, that doesn't mean that it actually exists. But Descartes' causal principle and theory of the degrees of reality circumvents this concern quite nicely. For an idea with the objective reality of Santa Claus, for example, is the idea of a finite being, and therefore it could be caused by a being with the formal reality of a finite substance, like the Meditator. As a result, the idea of Santa Claus does not imply that Santa Claus himself exists, because the Meditator could have invented it himself. So, given how the argument is set up, the only idea the Meditator cannot cause is the idea of an infinite substance, which just means that this argumentative tactic works only in the case of the idea of God and nothing else.

This, however, is not to say that the argument is flawless. On the contrary, in the *Third Objections*, the famous English empiricist philosopher, Thomas Hobbes, points out two major defects.

The first flaw concerns the theory that reality comes in degrees:

> Moreover, M. Descartes should consider afresh what 'more reality' means. Does reality admit of more and less? Or does he think one thing can be more of a thing than another? If so, he should consider how this can be explained to us with that degree of clarity that every demonstration calls for, and which he himself has employed elsewhere. (AT VII 185: CSM II 130)

Here the implication is that, without a clear and certain demonstration, there is no reason to believe that one thing is more real than something else, but rather either something is real or it is not real – period! Descartes' reply is just that he already showed that reality comes in degrees, and that it is self-evident (AT VII 185: CSM II 130). Many see this as mere hand-waving and not a legitimate response. However, in all fairness, Descartes believes that this was shown so clearly in the *Third Meditation* as to require no further proof. Why should he do it again? Indeed, all Hobbes has done is deny the claim without really addressing the reasons the Meditator gives for believing it.

However, something about this objection rings true. Why would anyone want to claim that reality comes in degrees? From a commonsense perspective, it does seem that something is either real or not, without degrees of more and less. This indicates another possible criticism. Notice that the only real effect of this doctrine is that an actual infinite substance must be the cause of the idea of an infinite substance. However, the doctrine does not have much work to do elsewhere. For no one could ever rationally suppose that some mode, like a shape, could cause the idea of a dog.[2] The issue just does not come up. Accordingly, it seems that the theory about reality coming in degrees is *ad hoc*; that is, it is invoked and employed merely for the sake of proving God's existence and nothing else. This could shed some serious doubt on the legitimacy of this doctrine. If it turns out that the doctrine is *ad hoc* and cannot stand on its own, then the entire argument would fall, because then nothing would preclude a finite thinking substance from being the cause of his idea of God.

The second defect centres on Hobbes' account of how a finite mind can come to have the idea of an infinite substance. Although Hobbes agrees that the idea of God does not originate in finite minds, he believes that 'it need not be derived from any source other than external objects' (AT VII 186: CSM II 131). Hobbes then proceeds to show how the conception of God as a supremely intelligent and powerful substance who is the creator of all things can be derived from the experience of material things existing external to the mind. Descartes gives the following reply:

> Nothing that we attribute to God can have been derived from external objects as a copy is derived from its original since nothing in God resembles what is to be found in external, that is corporeal things. Now any elements in our thought which do not resemble external objects manifestly cannot have originated in external objects, but must have come from the cause which produced this diversity in our thought. (AT VII 188: CSM II 132)

Here the idea of God's attributes cannot have come from corporeal things, because God is not himself corporeal and, therefore, the material world external to the mind does not resemble him in any way. Descartes goes on to wonder how the idea of God's understanding could have come from corporeal things, which cannot think and, therefore, cannot understand anything. He then elaborates as follows:

Now everyone surely perceives that there are things he understands. Hence everyone has the form or idea of understanding;
and by indefinitely extending this he can form the idea of God's
understanding. And a similar procedure applies to the other
attributes of God. (AT VII 188: CSM II 132)

In this passage, Descartes argues that the idea of God's understanding
is more likely to be derived from our idea of our own understanding
and then extending this idea indefinitely so that it reaches a point
where no limit can be determined. He then claims that the ideas of
the other attributes of God could be explained in a similar manner.

Although Descartes' response does seem to adequately defend
against this objection, it raises a serious question about the *Third
Meditation* arguments for God's existence. For recall that all of these
causal arguments rest upon the causal principle as it is applied to
ideas: any idea must receive its objective reality 'from some cause
which contains at least as much formal reality as there is objective
reality in the idea' (AT VII 41: CSM II 28). Given the doctrine that
reality comes in degrees, it follows that it is impossible for a finite substance or a mode to be the cause of the idea of God; only a being that
is formally or actually an infinite substance could be the cause of
such an idea. So if an example can be given of a finite mind creating
the idea of God, then this line of reasoning would fail, because a
finite thinking substance would not be ruled out as a possible cause
of this idea.

Hobbes' attempt to provide such an example seems to have failed
because of his reliance on corporeal things. However, other later
British philosophers such as John Locke and David Hume are in
agreement with Descartes to the extent that they look into their own
minds for the origin of this idea. Both Locke and Hume argued
against the existence of innate ideas and that all ideas must come
from experience. These ideas could then be 'compounded' with other
ideas, 'augmented' or 'distinguished'. This could occur in a variety
of different combinations. Hume gives the example of a golden mountain: one takes his idea of gold, his idea of a mountain, and then
combines or 'compounds' them to make the idea of a golden mountain. This reasoning can then be applied to the various attributes of
God. For example, someone could take her idea of her own power, say
of moving from place to place, and augment or increase it indefinitely. Next, she could indefinitely augment her idea of her own understanding, the idea of her own moral goodness, her own idea of love,

etc. Then once all of these ideas have been indefinitely augmented, she could combine or 'compound' them all together to make the idea of one, single being with all these attributes to the highest degree, i.e. a supremely perfect being.[3]

If this account is correct, then an example of how a finite mind could cause the idea of an infinite substance has been provided. This means that something that is not formally an infinite substance is the cause of the idea of an infinite substance. Hence, the causal principle, which is the lynchpin to all three causal arguments, is false. As a result, the Meditator cannot legitimately use this principle in his arguments and without it he cannot legitimately make the deductive move from the idea of God to the existence of God himself.

Before moving on, however, it is important to point out that Descartes did not shoot himself in the foot, nor was he being inconsistent in his retort to Hobbes. In fact, the Meditator has this to say about this kind of counter-example:

> [T]he unity, the simplicity, or the inseparability of all the attributes of God is one of the most important of the perfections which I understand him to have. And surely the idea of the unity of all his perfections could not have been placed in me by any cause which did not also provide me with the ideas of the other perfections . . . (AT VII 50: CSM II 34)

Here the Meditator is claiming that only a being with all these perfections united together so as to be utterly simple and, therefore, inseparable could have placed the idea of God in him. The gist is that the attribute of unity, simplicity or inseparability (which are all synonyms here) cannot be derived from any idea the Meditator has of himself or corporeal things. Those attributes, like supreme understanding and power, are separated by finite minds in their feeble attempt at understanding the divine essence. But in reality, all of God's attributes are not separate or distinct from each other. In fact, the simplicity of God's nature implies that what finite minds distinguish as separate perfections are really inseparable in God, because it is impossible for a simple thing (i.e. something without parts) to be divided into parts. Accordingly, the idea of God could not have been caused piecemeal from the mind's various ideas of different attributes, e.g. understanding, as Locke and Hume would later have it. Rather, the idea of God must have been caused in the mind whole and all at once so as to constitute 'the mark of the craftsman stamped on his work'.

4.4 THE ONTOLOGICAL ARGUMENT FOR GOD'S EXISTENCE

Descartes also employs an ontological argument for demonstrating God's existence. This kind of argument is not new to Descartes but was first formulated by the eleventh-century theologian and philosopher, Anselm of Canterbury. Although Descartes' rendering of the argument is somewhat different (and much simpler) than Anselm's, they share the same fundamental tactic – that an examination of the idea of God implies that God exists in reality. However, this kind of argument was seen as spurious even by Christian philosophers like Thomas Aquinas, who believed that the essence of God is not self-evident to human beings This raises a question about why Descartes bothered to include such a notoriously unconvincing argument in the first place.

Another important issue is the placement of the ontological argument in Descartes' works. In the *Principles*, it is found fairly early on at Part I, section 14, just before the causal arguments but after considerations about doubt and 'I think, therefore I am'. In the Geometric Exposition of the *Second Replies*, it is the first demonstration occurring after the customary list of definitions, axioms and postulates. However, in the *Meditations*, the ontological argument does not appear until the *Fifth Meditation*, which also discusses the nature of material things. So, not only is there a question as to why Descartes included it in the first place, but also the further question as to why he placed it in the various positions in these works. But before addressing these issues, it is important to understand the argument itself.

Perhaps the most accessible formulation of this argument is found in the following excerpt from the French edition of *Principles* I.14. After pointing out that the idea of a supremely perfect being stands out before the mind, he states:

> And [the mind] readily judges from what it perceives in this idea, that God, who is the supremely perfect being, is, or exists. For although it has distinct ideas of many other things it does not observe anything in them to guarantee the existence of their object. (AT VIIIA 10: CSM I 197)

The point here is that the mind observes something in the idea of God that guarantees his existence but the same is not the case for the ideas of other things. What is it that the mind specially observes in the idea of God? The answer is given straight away:

In this one idea the mind recognizes existence – not merely the possible and contingent existence which belongs to the ideas of all the other things which it distinctly perceives, but utterly necessary and eternal existence. (AT VIIIA 10: CSM I 197)

So, what the mind observes is that the idea of God contains the idea of necessary or eternal existence as contrasted with the possible or contingent existence observed in all other distinct ideas. 'Possible' or 'contingent' existence refers to the kind of existence contained in all distinct ideas besides that of God. To say that something exists 'contingently' is to say that the attributes contained in its idea do not imply a contradiction, and so God *could* bring it into existence if he so chose. For example, existence is contained in the idea of a unicorn to the extent that God could make such a creature if he so chose. But since unicorns do not exist, their existence is merely possible. This is also the case with actually existing creatures. For instance, possible or contingent existence is contained in the idea of a lion not because it could exist but doesn't, but because it is possible for lions not to exist. Now, while possible or contingent existence implies that something could exist or not, necessary or eternal existence precludes the possibility of not existing. In this way, it is impossible for a necessarily existing being not to exist. Since this is the case with the idea of God, it follows that he cannot not exist and, therefore, he *must* exist.

This is a very strong conclusion, especially considering that it is based on the mere inspection of the idea of God without recourse to anything else. In fact, Descartes believes that this line of reasoning is analogous to those employed in geometry:

Now on the basis of its perception that, for example, it is necessarily contained in the idea of a triangle that its three angles should equal two right angles, the mind is quite convinced that a triangle does have three angles equalling two right angles. (AT VIIIA 10: CSM I 197–8)

This deduction about triangles is the same kind of deduction as that made about God. In both cases, the mind can deduce something about the nature of the object under consideration. The conclusion that the three angles of a Euclidian triangle equals two right angles (i.e. 180 degrees) is derived from certain attributes constituting the nature of a triangle. Similarly, the conclusion that God necessarily exists is derived from the constitution of his nature as a supremely perfect being. Accordingly, the conclusion that God exists is just as certain as that about the angles of a triangle equalling two right angles.

Not everyone was convinced by this new, simpler and geometrically formulated version of Anselm's old argument. The author of the *First Objections*, the Dutch theologian Johan de Kater, who also went by the Latin name Johannes Caterus, raised two important objections. The first is that the argument only shows that the ideas of God and existence are inextricably linked and not that God actually exists outside the mind. The second is that the same line of reasoning can be used to prove that lions exist, because existence is contained in the concept 'existing lion' (AT VII 99–100: CSM II 72). Descartes addresses each of these objection in the *First Replies*.

His response to the first objection is that 'we are so accustomed to distinguishing existence from essence in the case of all other things that we fail to notice how closely existence belongs to essence in the case of God as compared with that of other things' (AT VII 116: CSM II 83). So, the attribute of actual (as opposed to possible) existence can be legitimately separated from the essence or nature of all created things. This is marked by the fact that any created thing can be consistently understood as not existing. For example, one can conceive of a world that is exactly as it is now but without lions ever existing in it. Notice that the nature or concept of a lion is in no way altered when conceived without existence. Indeed, it would still contain possible existence even though it did not actually exist. But, as Descartes pointed out, the same exercise cannot be performed with regards to God's nature, because a supremely perfect being cannot lack a perfection, viz. existence, and remain supremely perfect. So, even though everything else can be conceived as not existing, the same cannot be said in the unique case of God.

It is difficult to see how this is a response to Caterus' first objection. But Descartes' point seems to be that the inextricable link between God and existence is so different from that link in any other being that it somehow allows the move from existence being contained in the idea of God to his actual existence outside the mind. However, this response is far from adequate, for all Descartes has done is pointed out the special relation existence has with God's nature. This surely is not enough to permit an inference from the idea of God to his extra-mental existence. Furthermore, the special status accorded to existence with respect to God also raises the suspicion that it is *ad hoc*.

Descartes' response to Caterus' second objection is that 'we do not distinguish what belongs to the true and immutable essence of a thing from what is attributed to it merely by a fiction of the intellect' (AT VII 116: CSM II 83). Thus, people should be careful to focus their mental attention on the attributes that are really contained in a thing's true and immutable nature and be wary of mistakenly applying invented attributes to those natures. The criteria for determining whether or not the idea of a given nature is true and immutable or invented is based on the mind's ability or inability to separate the parts in question 'by a clear and distinct intellectual operation' (AT VII 117: CSM II 83). Descartes provides the following example:

> When, for example, I think of a winged horse or an actually existing lion or a triangle inscribed in a square, I readily understand that I am also able to think of a horse without wings, or a lion which does not exist, or a triangle apart from a square, and so on; hence these things do not have true and immutable natures. (AT VII 117: CSM II 84)

So, being winged, for example, is not part of the nature of a horse. This is marked by the fact that the mind can separate 'being winged' from its idea of a horse and still have the idea of a horse. The same thing happens when the mind separates the idea of actual existence from the nature of a lion, since lions can be understood as not existing. Accordingly, the idea of a winged horse is an invented nature, as is that of an 'existing lion'. But this same intellectual operation cannot be performed on the true and immutable natures of things. For example, the mind cannot separate the attribute of having three sides from the nature of a Euclidian triangle without turning it into the idea of something else, which is to destroy it. This also means that the real (i.e. non-invented) attributes of a true and immutable nature can be truthfully asserted about it. For example, the nature of a Euclidian triangle contains the attribute of its three angles equalling the sum of two right angles, and so this attribute can be truthfully asserted about or demonstrated from this nature.

These considerations apply to Caterus' second objection, that a line of reasoning similar to that of the ontological argument can be used to demonstrate the existence of lions from the idea of an 'existing lion'. Descartes' response is that the nature of an 'existing lion' is not true and immutable but invented as evidenced by the fact that a lion can be understood as not existing. This means that the true and immutable nature of a lion does not contain actual but only possible existence and, therefore, a lion's actual existence outside the mind cannot be legitimately demonstrated from it. However, the attribution of necessary existence to the nature of a supremely perfect being or God is not invented but truthfully asserted about it. For if the mind were to separate necessary existence from such a nature, then it would no longer be the nature of a supremely perfect being, but the nature of a being with all perfections except one. Therefore, according to Descartes, God's actual existence is legitimately deduced from his true and immutable nature as a supremely perfect being, while the same deduction cannot be made from the idea of an 'existing lion', because such a nature is not true and immutable but merely invented.

Bearing these considerations in mind, some conjectures about the placement of the ontological argument in several of Descartes' works can now be addressed. Descartes' response to Caterus' first objection is hopelessly lacking. All he does is reinforce the claim that the ideas of existence and God are very closely and inextricably linked. But this close linkage does not mean that God actually exists outside the mind. Instead, it shows only that *if* God exists, then it is impossible for him not to exist, i.e. he necessarily exists. So, on this account, God's existence must be independently demonstrated so as to satisfy the condition expressed in the antecedent (i.e. the 'if' part) in order to make the further deduction that God's existence is necessary. Interestingly enough, this is precisely what Descartes could claim he did in the *Meditations*. Since he already independently demonstrated God's existence in the *Third Meditation*, the Meditator can legitimately reach the conclusion that God *necessarily* exists in the *Fifth*, which would be to show something *about* God's existence and not *that* he exists. However, showing that God's existence is necessary cannot be the sole motivation for Descartes' employment of the ontological argument, for it is found before the causal arguments in both the Geometrical Exposition of the *Second Replies* and in the *Principles*.

The ontological argument is the first proposition demonstrated in the Geometrical Exposition, which should not be any surprise given the synthetic manner of its demonstration. Recall that synthetic demonstrations are based on stipulated axioms, definitions and postulates, which are then employed in further demonstrations from cause to effect. Since God is the first cause of everything, it makes sense that a synthetic demonstration of his existence should come before everything else. However, the ontological argument is clearly out of place in the first part of the *Principles* since it comes after the 'I think, therefore I am' but before the causal arguments. Its placement here is perhaps due to the fact that the progression of the *Principles* is not as tightly restrained by the geometrical order of reasons as are the *Meditations*. Accordingly, this argument can be employed after showing that anything that is clearly and distinctly perceived like 'I think, therefore I am' is absolutely certain. Evidently Descartes sees the ontological argument as having the same epistemological status as the conclusion 'I am or exist' in that the negation of each is self-contradictory.

4.5 THE IMMORTALITY OF THE SOUL

Another Christian doctrine besides God's existence that Descartes considered amenable to rational demonstration is the immortality of the soul. The subtitle of the first edition of the *Meditations* claims that the existence of God and the immortality of the soul are demonstrated. However, Descartes is well aware that the soul's immortality is not demonstrated in this work, and so subsequent editions have a corrected subtitle showing that God's existence and only 'the distinction between the human soul and the body' are demonstrated. The absence of such an argument is somewhat surprising given his claim in the Dedicatory Letter that the immortality of the soul is better demonstrated by reason (or philosophy) than theology. Why doesn't Descartes give such an argument?

Descartes is explicit about the absence of this argument in the *Synopsis* to the *Meditations* where he states that he stops at the conclusion that the mind or soul is really distinct from the body (see 7.1 and 7.2 below) for two reasons:

> [F]irst because these arguments are enough to show that the decay of the body does not imply the destruction of the mind, and are hence enough to give mortals the hope of an after-life, and secondly because the premises which lead to the conclusion that the soul is immortal depend on an account of the whole of physics. (AT VII 13–14: CSM II 10)

This passage indicates that, although an argument for the soul's immortality is within the bounds of human reason, it is well beyond the scope of the work at hand. This is expressed in his second reason where he states that such a demonstration would 'depend on an account of the whole of physics'. This is a tall order indeed and leaves little wonder as to why Descartes did not attempt it. Another interesting point is found in the first reason, namely that the possibility of the mind or soul existing without a body provides people with 'the hope of an after-life'.

Notice that only 'hope' and not 'knowledge' of an after-life is provided. This is understandable since Descartes does not provide an absolutely certain demonstration of the soul's immortality. But on what is this 'hope' of an after-life based? Remember that Descartes only claims that the mind is really distinct from the body. As discussed at 3.1, this just means that it is possible for them to exist independently of one another at least by the power of God. So, the real distinction arguments only show that it is *possible* for the mind to exist without the body and not that it actually does. This possibility of independent existence is the basis for this hope in an after-life, for if it were demonstrated that the mind or soul is not really distinct from the body, then it would be impossible for the mind to exist without it. Descartes mentions in the Dedicatory Letter that some people have come to this conclusion based on rational arguments but believe by faith that the soul is immortal (AT VII 3: CSM II 4). These people would then hold contradictory beliefs, which is irrational. So, in demonstrating the real distinction between mind and body, Descartes is bringing this Christian doctrine into accord with reason, thereby re-establishing a rational hope in a life after bodily death.

However, even though Descartes never explicitly gives an argument for the soul's immortality, he hints at one in a letter dated August 1641 to an unknown correspondent going by the name of 'Hyperaspites' (which is the Greek word for 'champion'). In this letter Descartes claims that 'a human, being a composite entity, is naturally corruptible, while the mind is incorruptible and immortal' (AT III 422: CSM K 189). Thus, a human being is a composite of mind and body. Accordingly, the whole human being is corruptible in that these two parts can be separated. This doctrine is also applied to the body. The human body results from the configuration and motion of material parts (see AT VII 14: CSM II 10). The body dies when some of these parts decay or cease to function properly (see 7.8). But since corruptibility requires an entity composed of parts that can be separated, the soul's lack of parts makes it incorruptible. Using this basic line of reasoning, Descartes concludes that 'while the body can very easily perish, the mind is immortal by its very nature' (AT VII 14: CSM II 10).

This, however, only means that the soul is naturally incorruptible in that the soul would not cease to exist in the normal course of nature. But this still does not constitute a demonstration where the soul's immortality is established with absolute certainty. This is because any substance, including thinking substances, minds or souls, can be 'reduced to nothingness by God's denying his concurrence to them' (AT VII 14: CSM II 10). This means that it is always possible for the human soul to cease to exist if God so chose. Descartes also mentions this limitation of his proof in the following succinct excerpt from a letter of 24 December 1640 to Mersenne:

> I could not prove that God could not annihilate the soul, but only that it is by nature entirely distinct from the body, and consequently it is not bound by nature to die with it. This is all that is required as a foundation for religion, and is all that I had any intention of proving. (AT III 266: CSM K 163)

So, in the end, Descartes never does demonstrate that the soul is immortal but only that it is naturally incorruptible and will continue to exist after the corruption of the body as long as God chooses not to annihilate it.[4] Therefore, humans have good reason to hope for an after-life.

4.6 THE EUCHARIST

The Catholic Church teaches that the bread and wine distributed at communion actually change into the body and blood of Christ while still maintaining the appearance of bread and wine. This literal understanding of Jesus' words at the Last Supper means for Catholics that a miracle happens at every Mass. The way in which the miracle was supposed to happen was considered one of the mysteries of the faith, and so it technically falls outside the scope of reason as laid out by Descartes. However, the author of the *Fourth Objections*, Fr Antoine Arnauld, notices a tension between Descartes' philosophy and the traditional account of how God performs this miracle:

> But what I see as likely to give the greatest offence to theologians is that according to the author's doctrines it seems that the Church's teaching concerning the sacred mysteries of the Eucharist cannot remain completely intact.

We believe on faith that the substance of the bread is taken away from the bread of the Eucharist and only the accidents remain. These are extension, shape, colour, smell, taste and other qualities perceived by the senses. (AT VII 217: CSM II 152–3)

Arnauld indicates the point of conflict as being a result of both Descartes' claim that there are no sensible qualities, such as colour, smell and taste, in things themselves and the claim that shape, motion, etc. are modes that cannot exist apart from a substance. (See 3.1 and 3.2.)

Arnauld's point in the second paragraph provides a broad description of the accepted view among theologians of the time, which goes back as far as Thomas Aquinas. Broadly speaking, the bread and the wine were thought to really become the body and blood of Christ upon consecration by the priest, while the smell, taste, colour, shape, size, etc. of the bread and wine remain. But at communion, the bread is not shaped like Jesus' body but like a wafer. It also smells and tastes like a wafer. This raises the question of how the substance or essence of the bread can be the body of Christ while it smells, tastes and looks like a wafer. The answer posed by Aquinas and later scholastics, such as Francisco Suarez, was that the properties or (more technically speaking) accidents of the bread remain while the substance or essence of the bread literally changed into the body of Christ. Hence, since the accidents of the bread remain, it looks, smells and tastes like bread when it is in its essence the body of Christ.

This means that the miracle of the Eucharist consists in God doing two things at once. The first is to change the essence of bread into the essence of Jesus' body. The second is to sustain the existence of the shape, size, smell and taste of the wafer despite the fact that the essence of the bread is now gone. These kinds of accidents that can exist without a substance, at least by the power of God, came to be known as 'real accidents'.[5] These real accidents were, so to speak, the 'clothing' that gave the appearance of bread to something that was essentially or substantially the body of Christ. As a result, before consecration the priest has something that is a wafer in both its essence (i.e. it really is a wafer) and its accidents (it has the size, shape, taste and smell of a wafer); but after the consecration the priest now has something that is essentially different, viz. the body of Christ, but continues to have the accidents of the wafer so that it still looks and tastes like a wafer.

Arnauld indicated a twofold point of conflict between Descartes' philosophy and this traditional account, namely Descartes' denial of sensible qualities, like colour, smell and taste, and his claim that modes cannot exist without a substance. For Descartes, sensible qualities such as colour, smell and taste are not found in things themselves but are mere ideas in the mind caused by the configuration and motion of the microscopic material parts found in particular things. For example, a lemon does not contain the quality of 'sourness' which is then transferred to the mind through the sense organ of taste, as the scholastic-Aristotelian tradition seemed to maintain. Instead, the sensory idea of sour that arises when a lemon is tasted is caused by the shape, size, motion and configuration of the microscopic particles in the lemon and their mechanistic interaction with the microscopic particles making up the taste buds on the tongue. Hence, according to Descartes, all sensible qualities such as these are reducible to the quantifiable properties of extension, like shape, size, motion and their configuration.

But these modes of extension cannot exist apart from an extended substance, at least insofar as humans are able to comprehend God's power. For the intellectual perception of a mode cannot be fully excluded from that of its underlying substance. This inability to fully exclude one idea from another indicates that the former depends on the latter for its existence. This doctrine of modes, therefore, precludes the possibility of the 'real accidents' traditionally used by theologians to explain the miracle of the Eucharist. This is made explicit in the *Sixth Replies*:

> In order to demolish the doctrine of the reality of accidents, I do not think we need to look for any arguments beyond those I have already deployed ... [I]t is completely contradictory that there should be real accidents, since whatever is real can exist separately from any other subject; yet anything that can exist separately in this way is a substance, not an accident. (AT VII 434: CSM II 293)

Here Descartes attacks the notion of a 'real accident' as being self-contradictory. An accident is, by definition, something that ultimately resides in some substance. But the claim that these accidents are 'real' implies that they can exist without residing in an underlying substance, at least by the power of God; that is, it is really distinct from its underlying substance and would, therefore, be a substance in its own right. Hence, a real accident would be something that both does and does not require residence in a substance, which is contradictory.[6] As a result, Descartes cannot explain the Eucharist by recourse to real accidents as his scholastic-Aristotelian counterparts traditionally did.

Descartes actually sidesteps the issue in the *Fourth Replies* when, after giving a fairly detailed account of a body's surface and how sensation occurs by either direct or indirect (i.e. through the air) contact with a surface, he notes that his doctrine of surfaces is consistent with the canons on this topic issued by the Council of Trent, and that these canons do not require that the Eucharist be explained by real accidents (AT VII 251: CSM II 175). In a letter to Mesland dated 9 February 1645, Descartes claims that he made this reference in order to excuse himself from giving such an explanation, since he is not a professional theologian (AT IV 165: CSM 242). However, Descartes gives a more detailed account of his views on the Eucharist later in this letter but only:

> on condition that if you [Mesland] communicate it to anyone else you will please not attribute its authorship to me; and on condition that you do not communicate it to anyone at all unless you judge it to be altogether in accord with what has been laid down by the Church. (A IV 1165: CSM K 242)

So, even though Descartes finally does figure out a solution to this theological difficulty, he is very reluctant to make his theory public for fear of coming into controversy with Catholic theologians. But he goes on to give his explanation anyway.

Descartes preambles his discussion with an account of the term 'human body'. He argues that this term is ambiguous between the parts of matter or extension constituting a human body and a body that is substantially united to a human mind or soul. The gist is that a 'human body' in the first sense is not exactly the same after some part of its extension has been lost or changed. So, a human body in this sense is identified with the extension constituting it. Accordingly, if a 'human body' in this sense were to lose some piece of extension (say, a finger) or if some aspect of its configuration were to change, it would no longer be the same body as before but something different. But a 'human body' in the second sense of the word as substantially united to a human soul remains exactly the same if some of its extension is lost or changed. The reason for this is that it is still one and the same soul that is united to this body to form one thing. For example, if a living human being, let's call her 'Jane', loses a finger, her body remains the same human body (in this second, more strict sense) despite the fact that she has lost some of her extension, because it is still the same living human body as before, i.e. it is still Jane's body. The aim here seems to be that, strictly speaking, a human body is a living human body, i.e. a body that is substantially united to a human mind or soul, while a 'human body' in the first sense of a mere configuration of parts is either to abstract this aspect of a living human being and consider it under the general idea of extension or it applies to non-living human bodies or corpses. (See AT IV 166–8: CSM K 242–3.)[7]

Descartes then goes on to utilize the manner in which the identity of the human body in the second and stricter sense of the term depends on the soul in his account of the Eucharist. His position seems to be that, upon consecration, the whole of Jesus' soul is supernaturally (i.e. by a miracle and not in the usual course of nature) united with the wafer such that it is wholly in the whole wafer and wholly in each and every one of its particles. This latter point about the whole in the whole and the whole in each of its parts was a standard way of describing how the soul is united to a human body, which will be discussed in more detail at 7.8. But for present purposes the point is that the wafer is now the 'body of Christ', because it is the body to which Jesus' soul is now united (see AT IV 168: CSM K 244). For example, the body that is Jane's is hers precisely because it is the body to which Jane herself, i.e. her mind or soul, is substantially united. The same is true of the wafer in the Eucharist: the wafer is the body possessed by Jesus due to his substantial union with it. Accordingly, the wafer is now the 'body of Christ' in that it is the body possessed by Jesus himself.

This is quite a slick way around a very sticky issue. For notice that Descartes does not make any reference to the wafer as a body in the first sense of the word, i.e. as a configuration of extended parts, but only to the wafer as a body in the second, stricter sense. This then allows him to play with the possessive 'of' in the phrase 'body of Christ'. The 'of' here, as Descartes seems to understand it, means just any body possessed by Jesus. Now, since Jesus is identical to his mind or soul (unique as it is), it follows that any body to which his soul is united would be in his possession and, therefore, it would be 'the body of Christ'. This is precisely what Descartes is doing with his account of the Eucharist. The wafer is 'the body of Christ' just because it is the body to which Jesus himself is united by supernatural power after the consecration.

In concluding this chapter, a moment should be taken to recognize the integral role of religion in Descartes' philosophical system. Unlike today when religion and science are often thought to be mutually exclusive domains of human thought, the existence of God actually supports Descartes' epistemological and scientific projects, for not only does Descartes use the nature and existence of God to ground his fundamental laws of motion (see 6.7), but he also, and more importantly, uses God's existence and his non-deceiving nature to secure his absolutely certain foundation for knowledge. This epistemological function is crucial for Descartes, because without it no absolutely certain knowledge could ever be achieved in the sciences. An interesting implication of this is that people who do not know that God exists cannot have scientific knowledge. The next chapter turns to this notion of scientific knowledge or *scientia* and how Descartes believes it can be attained.

CHAPTER 5

KNOWLEDGE

Now that the roots are firmly in place, it is time to see how they actually secure the philosophical tree. This chapter is devoted to Descartes' theory of knowledge and some of the issues arising from it. The main issues to be discussed will be why people make mistakes, how to avoid them, and how God's existence and non-deceiving nature guarantee the truth of what is clearly and distinctly perceived. Moreover, Descartes' proof of an external world is used as an illustration of how God's guarantee works; and finally the claim that the reasoning of the *Meditations* does not really follow the geometrical order but is circular is examined.

5.1 SCIENTIA

It is important at the outset to be clear about the nature of Descartes' epistemological project. What is here being called 'knowledge' is just the English translation of the Latin *scientia*, which is also the root for the English word 'science'. For Descartes, *scientia* denotes an interconnected system of knowledge. This harks back to the discussion of the four rules of Descartes' method laid out in Part II of the *Discourse* where an order is supposed 'even among objects that have no natural order or precedence.' This indicates Descartes' belief that all knowledge is interconnected in such a way that each object is knowable by way of a deduction from something else. The trick is to be patient and to 'ascend little by little, step by step.' So, Descartes' goal is to guarantee the absolute certainty of the connection between links in the deductive chain in order to obtain systematic knowledge of these interconnected truths.

Recall further that one of Descartes' biggest problems with the traditional scholastic-Aristotelian method was the probable nature of its reasoning. He was very put off by the fact that these philosophers could not agree on anything and were constantly engaged in controversy. Descartes attributed this tendency for disagreement to the fact that probable syllogisms leave room for other, probable theories. As a result, someone's opinion could change with the introduction of any new argument. This fuelled his desire for conclusions based on absolutely certain foundations, which would exclude probable alternatives. This exclusion would also cut off the possibility for error and controversy. So, the search for *scientia* is not only an attempt at finding secure truths but it is also an attempt to avoid error and falsehood.

5.2 FORMAL AND MATERIAL FALSITY

Interestingly enough, Descartes does not say very much about truth. But he does spend a lot of time examining the nature of error and falsehood. Since falsehood is the opposite of truth, an examination of falsehood should help provide an account of Descartes' understanding of truth and how error can be avoided. Let's begin with the following excerpt from the *Third Meditation*:

> Now as far as ideas are concerned, provided they are considered solely in themselves and I do not refer them to anything else, they cannot strictly speaking be false; for whether it is a goat or a chimera I am imagining, it is just as true that I imagine the former as the latter. (AT VII 37: CSM II 26)

This passage claims that ideas in and of themselves, without reference to anything external to them, cannot be false. The examples of the ideas of a goat and of a chimera are helpful, for goats exist but chimeras do not. Considered in themselves as ideas in the mind, they cannot be false, because it is true that they exist as ideas, e.g. it is true that 'I' am imagining a goat at one time and a chimera at another. Thus truth and falsehood are not found in the ideas themselves but only when the mind refers those ideas to a state of affairs. So, even the idea of a chimera cannot be false unless it is referred to the world outside the mind.

After making a similar point about emotions and desires, Descartes decides:

> Thus the only remaining thoughts where I must be on my guard against making a mistake are judgements. And the chief and most

common mistake which is to be found here consists in my judging that the ideas which are in me resemble, or conform to, things located outside me. (AT VII 37: CSM II 26)

Hence, only judgements give rise to mistakes, and these occur when it is affirmed that some idea resembles or conforms to something existing outside the mind. For example, suppose Joe judges that this animal at the zoo is an ostrich. But, as it turns out, Joe has made a mistake: it is really an emu. Notice that falsehood and error arose because of Joe's judgement that his idea conformed to the world outside his mind when it did not. This also suggests that truth occurs when one judges that an idea conforms to the world when it, in fact, does.

Descartes calls this lack of conformity between the idea and the world 'formal falsity'. However, Descartes also speaks of another, more controversial species of falsehood called 'material falsity', which occurs when ideas 'represent non-things as things' (AT VII 43: CSM II 30). This indicates that the idea of a chimera, though not formally false, is materially false since it represents something that does not exist (i.e. a non-thing) as a thing that does exist. Descartes uses the ideas of hot and cold as examples. He claims that these ideas are so obscure that he cannot tell if heat is the absence of cold or vice versa.

And since there can be no ideas which are not as it were of things, if it is true that cold is nothing but the absence of heat, the idea which represents it to me as something real and positive deserves to be called false; and the same goes for other ideas of this kind. (AT VII 44: CSM II 30)

If heat, for instance, is the absence of cold, then it is not really anything positive but a mere lack or absence of something, which is to say that it is nothing at all. But the idea of heat represents this non-thing as though it were a thing or positive reality existing outside the mind, in things themselves. For Descartes, the ideas of other sensible qualities like colour and taste discussed at 4.6 are also materially false for the same reason: they represent colours and tastes as existing in the things themselves when they do not.

Arnauld, in the *Fourth Objections*, raises two issues about the legitimacy of the doctrine of material falsity. The first concerns the distinction between it and formal falsity:

What is the idea of cold? It is coldness itself in so far as it exists objectively in the intellect. But if cold is an absence, it cannot exist objectively in the intellect by means of an idea whose object-ive existence is a positive entity. Therefore, if cold is merely an absence, there cannot ever be a positive idea of it, and hence there cannot be an idea which is materially false. (AT VII 206: CSM II 145)

This passage harks back to Descartes' causal principle that some-thing cannot come from nothing. Hence, if the objective reality of the idea of cold is something positive, then it could not have been caused by an absence, which is, strictly speaking, nothing. This leads to the second issue: even though cold may not be some-thing positive, it is still true that the idea of cold represents some positive reality to the mind. Therefore, 'the idea in question may perhaps not be the idea of cold, but it cannot be a false idea' (AT VII 207: CSM II 145). Thus, although the idea would not in fact be the idea of cold but of something else, it is not false because of this. Rather, any falsehood is the result of the judgement that it is the idea of cold when it really is not. Hence, since judgement is the culprit, the falsehood of the idea of cold must be formal and not material.

Descartes responds that Arnauld's objections deal only with the objective reality of an idea, which is to focus on its formal aspect alone. But the doctrine of material falsity concerns them only as ideas in the mind, which is in their material aspect. Both agree that, strictly speaking, falsehood is found only in judgements. But Descartes departs from Arnauld when he argues that materially false ideas are not false in this way but only in a very loose sense of the term. Rather, an idea is materially false only to the extent that it provides *material* for error due to its inaccurate representation of things existing outside the mind, and so they are not false in the strict or formal sense (AT VII 232: CSM II 162–3).[1]

Descartes' response, however, does not really address the concern about how the objective reality of cold, for example, can be caused by nothing. However, this challenge can be met through the doctrine that such sensible qualities are produced by the size, shape and motion of microscopic bodily parts. This means that something positive is causing the ideas of heat, colour, taste, etc. but that the resulting objective reality does not accurately represent its cause. This lies at the heart of the claim that materially false ideas provide material for error, since they represent sensible qualities as things not resembling or conforming to what is really there. Formal falsity occurs when the judgement is made that the sourness people taste, for example, is found in the lemon, because what is represented objectively in the idea does not resemble or conform to the reality of the situation. In this way, the sensory idea of sourness provides the material for making that mistake. Hence, material falsity makes formal falsity or error more likely to occur. The question then becomes: how can people reliably avoid making these mistakes even though some of their ideas are materially false?

5.3 GOD'S NON-DECEIVING NATURE

For Descartes, the first step toward the reliable avoidance of error is the knowledge that God cannot be a deceiver. The argument that God cannot be a deceiver is found at the end of the *Third* and at the beginning of the *Fourth Meditation* as well as at *Principles* I.29. The formulation found in the *Fourth Meditation* is as follows:

> I recognize that it is impossible that God should ever deceive me. For in every case of trickery or deception some imperfection is to be found; and although the ability to deceive appears to be an indication of cleverness or power, the will to deceive is undoubtedly evidence of malice or weakness, and so cannot apply to God. (AT VII 53: CSM II 37)

So, since God is an all-perfect being, he cannot have any imperfections. But the desire or will to deceive is malicious in nature and so it is an imperfection. Therefore God cannot have the will to deceive. As a result, it is impossible for God to be a deceiver.

Yet, despite this conclusion, there are instances in the Bible where God does seem to deceive humans. Descartes makes the following response to this objection in the *Second Replies*:

> As everyone knows, there are two quite distinct ways of speaking about God. The first is appropriate for ordinary understanding and does contain some truth, albeit truth which is relative to human beings; and it is this way of speaking that is generally employed in Holy Scripture. The second way of speaking comes closer to expressing the naked truth ... it is the way of speaking that everyone ought to use when philosophizing, and that I had a

special obligation to use in my *Meditations* . . . (AT VII 142: CSM II 102)

In this passage, Descartes distinguishes between a manner of speaking about God that is accessible to everyone and a manner of speaking that is more technical and reserved for professional philosophers and theologians. The first, more popular way of speaking is found in the Bible. Accordingly, God's will may be expressed as though he deceived some person or prophet, but in the stricter, more philosophical way of speaking, this just cannot be so. For recall that the argument is not based on the act of deception but on the maliciousness entailed by the *will* to deceive:

> I would not want to criticize those who allow that through the mouths of the prophets God can produce verbal untruths which, like the lies of doctors who deceive their patients in order to cure them, are free of any malicious intent to deceive. (AT VII 143: CSM II 102)

Here Descartes acknowledges that God has allowed his prophets to speak falsehoods, but since God is doing this for our own good, as a doctor might lie to his patient or a parent to her child, there is no malicious intent. Therefore, God is said to lie in the Bible for the sake of popular understanding; however, the absence of malicious intent means that God, in the more technical sense, did not have the will to deceive. Accordingly, these counter-examples from the Bible do not undermine the conclusion that God cannot be a deceiver.

5.4 THE SOURCE OF ERROR

Now with the theses of God's existence and his non-deceiving nature in place, it is important to understand Descartes' explanation of how errors occur in order to understand his method for avoiding them and attaining absolutely certain knowledge. Descartes' first concern in this regard is to place the responsibility for mistakes squarely on the finite minds who make them. In the *Fourth Meditation*, the Meditator acknowledges that he is not aware of any faculty for generating errors, which raises two important points. First, this precludes the possibility of God being the cause of human error. For if he had a God-given faculty for making mistakes, then God would ultimately be responsible for those mistakes since he was the origin of the faculty itself. Moreover, if God did give him such a faculty without his being aware of it, then God would be a deceiver, which is impossible. Hence, God cannot be the source of the Meditator's mistakes.

Secondly, since error does not have God as its author, then it is not a positive being but a lack, for 'error is not a pure negation, but rather a privation or lack of some knowledge which somehow should be in me' (AT VII 55: CSM II 38). A mistake is a 'privation' in the sense that 'I' ought to have some knowledge that 'I' am missing, whereas a mere negation of knowledge is just ignorance. For example, scientists are ignorant as to whether or not life exists on other planets. This is a mere negation of knowledge – scientists just don't know. But people today who still believe (or claim to believe) that the earth is not round but flat are not ignorant but are making a mistake, because they lack a piece of knowledge that they should have. This means that the idea they have of the earth is formally false, because the idea of a flat earth does not resemble or conform to reality. Hence, error is not a mere lack of knowledge, but rather it is knowledge that 'I' should have but don't.

But how is it that 'I' miss some bit of knowledge that 'I' should have? The answer to this question entails a slightly more detailed explanation of the faculty of judgment, which is the result of the interplay between intellect and will. Recall from 2.3 that the intellect is the faculty of understanding and the will is the faculty of voluntary choice whereby certain propositions are chosen to be affirmed or denied and certain objects are chosen to be pursued or avoided. The intellect is, of course, limited in that not everything is understood, while God's intellect is unlimited in that he does understand everything. The will, however, 'can in a certain sense be called infinite, since we observe without exception that its scope extends to anything that can possibly be an object of any other will – even the immeasurable will of God' (AT VIIIA 18: CSM I 204).[2] Hence, the scope of the will extends much further than the scope of the intellect.

This asymmetry between intellect and will is what gives rise to mistakes. The intellect's job is to present things to the will so that it can make its choices. But, since the will extends beyond the bounds of the intellectual perception, it can choose to affirm or deny something that is not firmly within the bounds of the understanding. So, mistakes happen when a proposition that is not sufficiently understood by the intellect is affirmed or denied by the will. When this happens, a choice is made that should not have been made due to the insufficient understanding of the issue at hand. Therefore, mistakes are a result of the choices that 'I' make, and so 'I', and not God, am responsible for 'my' own mistakes. Rather, since God is the author of these faculties, they are perfect within their kind and mistakes are a result of 'my' misuse of them.

However, one might object that God could have given people an intellect that was not finite but infinite or, at least, one that was wider in scope than the faculty currently possessed. This would then be another way in which God could be the cause of human error. A response to this concern can be extrapolated from the following:

> It also occurs to me that whenever we are inquiring whether the works of God are perfect, we ought to look at the whole universe, not just at one created thing on its own. For what would perhaps rightly appear very imperfect if it existed on its own is quite perfect when its function as a part of the universe is considered. (AT VII 55–6; CSM II 39)

Here the Meditator says that something may appear very imperfect when considered all by itself and removed from its function as part of the universe. However, when that same thing is considered as part of the universe, it is easy to see how perfect it is in its contribution to the whole. It can be inferred from this that the finitude of the intellect is seen as imperfect when considered by itself. But if it could be seen how it, along with the possibility of error, functions as part of God's universe, then it could be seen how it is perfect in fulfilling its function as part of the whole. Accordingly, 'I cannot produce any reason to prove that God ought to have given me a greater faculty of knowledge than he did . . .' (AT VII 56: CSM II 39); '[a]nd I have no cause for complaint . . . Indeed, I have reason to give thanks to him who has never owed me anything for the great bounty that he has shown me, rather than thinking myself deprived or robbed of any gifts he did not bestow' (AT VII 60: CSM II 42). Therefore, the fact that God did not give people a broader understanding does not make him responsible for their mistakes. Instead, people should be thankful that they have any understanding at all, limited though it may be, and they should take responsibility for the free choices involved in making judgements.

5.5 HOW TO AVOID ERROR AND GOD'S GUARANTEE

It is important to remember that in the *Meditations* Descartes (through the Meditator) is not looking for probable knowledge, which is only certain to the degree that it is likely. Since this likelihood does not provide any guarantee, there is always the possibility of error. The Meditator then argues that error can be avoided and absolutely certain knowledge can be achieved by choosing to affirm or deny only those propositions that the intellect clearly and distinctly perceives. Descartes explains what he means by a 'clear and distinct perception' at *Principles* I.45:

> I call a perception 'clear' when it is present and accessible to the attentive mind – just as we say that we see something clearly when it is present to the eye's gaze and stimulates it with a sufficient degree of strength and accessibility. (AT VIIIA 21–2: CSM I 207)

This explanation of the clarity of a given perception harks back to 1.3 where Descartes' doctrine of intuition was discussed. Recall that a truth is perceived by intuition when it is clearly and distinctly perceived all at once and in one, sweeping mental gaze. Hence, the object of the intellect's perception should be in such sharp intellectual focus that all aspects of it are plainly evident to anyone paying attention to it. Moreover, an idea is 'distinct' to the extent that it is clearly distinguished or marked off from other ideas. So, clear and distinct ideas are not confused with one another, and they are in sharp intellectual focus.

In the early *Regulae*, Descartes seems to believe that the certainty of clear and distinct perception found in intuition was so obvious that it required no further justification. However, in his later works, such as the *Meditations* and *Principles*, Descartes recognizes a need for securing their absolute certainty. This security is provided by God's non-deceiving nature:

> Its author [i.e. the author of clear and distinct perceptions], I say, is God, who is supremely perfect, and who cannot be a deceiver on pain of contradiction; hence the perception is undoubtedly true. (AT VII 62: CSM II 43)

Descartes gives a slightly more thorough account at *Principles* I.43:

I say that this is certain, because God is not a deceiver, and so the faculty of perception which he has given us cannot incline to falsehood; and the same goes for the faculty of assent, provided its scope is limited to what is clearly perceived. (AT VIIIA 21: CSM I 207)

In both passages, the Meditator and Descartes explicitly state that God's non-deceiving nature guarantees the truth of all clear and distinct perceptions. The second passage elaborates on this: the God-given faculty of perception or intellect must tend towards truth, for if it tended towards falsehood, God would be a deceiver, which is impossible. Descartes continues:

And even if there were no way of proving this, the minds of all of us have been so moulded by nature that whenever we perceive something clearly, we spontaneously give our assent to it and are quite unable to doubt its truth. (AT VIIIA 21: CSM I 207)

Here Descartes states that people automatically assent to or affirm clear and distinct perceptions and that they cannot legitimately be called into doubt. This last remark sheds some light on how God's non-deceiving nature guarantees the truth of clear and distinct perceptions. The fact that people cannot help but affirm their truth without doubt indicates that if they were mistaken about their clear and distinct perceptions, there would be no way to discover the mistake. If this were true, then God would have created humans so that they could not help but think something was true when in fact it was false. On this account, God would have deceived them into thinking that something is true with absolute certainty (since it cannot honestly be called it into doubt) when in fact it is false. But the fact that God cannot be a deceiver precludes this scenario. Therefore, all clear and distinct perceptions must be true on pain of contradicting God's non-deceiving nature.[3]

Accordingly, error can be avoided if people make judgements only about those ideas that are clear and distinct. This is because God guarantees the truth of clear and distinct perceptions, and therefore judgements about them cannot be wrong. Moreover, people should abstain from making judgements about ideas that are not clear and distinct, for the absence of God's guarantee leaves room for doubt and formal falsehood. One might object that it is still possible to make true judgements even without God's guarantee. The Meditator responds to this as follows:

> [I]f in such cases I either affirm or deny, then I am not using my free will correctly. If I go for the alternative which is false, then obviously I shall be in error; if I take the other side, then it is by pure chance that I arrive at the truth, and I shall still be at fault since it is clear by the natural light that the perception of the intellect should always precede the determination of the will. (AT VII 59–60: CSM II 41)

This passage first states that if falsehood is chosen, then clearly the person is at fault for her mistake. But it also states that even if the truth is chosen, the person who chose to affirm or deny it without a clear and distinct perception is still blameworthy. This is because 'the perception of the intellect should always precede the determination of the will.' In other words, the correct use of the will in choosing to affirm or deny (or pursue or avoid) something requires that the object be sufficiently perceived by the intellect, for it is not responsible to make decisions about things about which not enough is understood. This would be to throw the dice with the hopes of achieving knowledge by luck and not by a reliable method for seeking and discovering the truth. So, in the end, the way to avoid error is to make choices to affirm or deny *only* those perceptions that are clear and distinct and to abstain from making such a choice about anything that is not.[4]

5.6 PROOF OF AN EXTERNAL WORLD

The proofs of a world of bodies existing outside the mind laid out in the *Sixth Meditation* and Part II of the *Principles* provide a very nice example of how God's non-deceiving nature works in obtaining absolutely certain knowledge.[5] This argument is much like the main argument for God's existence in the *Third Meditation* in that Descartes or the Meditator begins with the existence of certain kinds of ideas, enumerates the possible causes of those ideas, and then reaches his conclusion by a process of elimination. In the case of bodies, the existence of ideas with the objective reality of bodily things is acknowledged. The question then becomes: what is the cause of these ideas? The cause of these ideas could be either (1) 'me', i.e. the Meditator or Descartes himself, (2) God, (3) a creature more noble than a body (e.g. an angel), or (4) the bodies themselves. The Meditator or Descartes then proceeds to eliminate all but one of these possibilities.

The first option is eliminated, because sensory ideas are not in his control in that he cannot will that one sensation (e.g. smelling flowers) occurs rather than another (e.g. smelling a skunk); that is, these ideas are adventitious and, therefore, they are received passively without any action (i.e. will) on his part (see AT VII 79: CSM II 55; and AT VIIIA 40: CSM I 223). This means that 'another substance distinct from me – a substance which contains either formally or eminently all the reality which exists objectively in the ideas produced by this faculty' must be the cause of these ideas (AT VII 79: CSM II 55). Notice that options (2) to (4) satisfy this criterion, for all of them are either formally material things, i.e. the bodies themselves, or things that are not bodies but contain that reality in a higher form, i.e. God and angels.

Options (2) God and (3) a creature more noble than a body are then ruled out because of the previous considerations about God's non-deceiving nature. This is expressed quite nicely in the following excerpt from the *Sixth Meditation*:

> But since God is not a deceiver, it is quite clear that he does not transmit the ideas to me either directly from himself, or indirectly, via some creature which contains the objective reality of the ideas not formally but eminently. For God has given me no faculty at all for recognizing any such source for these ideas . . . (AT VII 79: CSM II 55)

Here the Meditator explicitly employs God's non-deceiving nature to rule out those options wherein the reality contained in the ideas of bodies would be contained only eminently in their causes, i.e. options (2) and (3). This is because he could not come to realize that God or an angel, for example, was in fact the cause of his ideas of bodily things. In fact:

> [God] has given me a great propensity to believe that they are produced by corporeal things. So I do not see how God could be understood to be anything but a deceiver if the ideas were transmitted from a source other than corporeal things. It follows that corporeal things exist. (AT VII 79–80: CSM II 55)

So God gave him a strong inclination for believing that ideas of bodily things come from things that are formally or actually bodies extended in length, breadth and depth. Furthermore, God has not provided him with any way of discovering whether or not this inclination or propensity is mistaken, which would mean that God is a deceiver. But, since this is impossible, neither God nor a creature more noble than a body like an angel or a deceiving god could be the cause of the ideas of bodily things. Therefore, the only remaining option is that (4) bodies themselves, i.e. things that are formally extended in length, breadth and depth, must be the cause of the ideas of bodily things.

5.7 THE CARTESIAN CIRCLE

The title of this section, 'The Cartesian Circle', is the name scholars commonly give to what is seen as a central fault of the *Meditation*'s entire epistemological project, viz. that the Meditator reasons in a vicious circle. Circular reasoning is considered fallacious because one or more of the premises assumes the truth of the conclusion. For example, if the conclusion that God exists were based on the premise that the Bible says so, then the argument would be circular, because the Bible is supposed to be the word of God, which in turn means that God must exist in order for him to say anything that is recorded in the Bible. Hence, in this case, the premise 'The Bible says that God exists' assumes what it is trying to prove, viz. that God exists. The whole of the *Meditations* has been accused of this sort of bad reasoning since before its publication.

In fact, several of the people from whom Descartes solicited objections before the publication of the *Meditations* raise this point. Perhaps the clearest expression of this criticism is found in the *Fourth Objections*:

> I have one further worry, namely how the author avoids reasoning in a circle when he says that we are sure that what we clearly and distinctly perceive is true only because God exists.
>
> But we can be sure that God exists only because we clearly and distinctly perceive this. Hence, before we can be sure that God exists, we ought to be able to be sure that whatever we perceive clearly and evidently is true. (AT VII 214: CSM II 150)

Here Arnauld is saying that the certainty of clear and distinct perceptions rests, as has been said, on the conclusions that God exists and that he cannot be a deceiver. Yet each of the premises in the *Third Meditation* arguments for God's existence is supposed to be clear and distinct and, therefore, certain. But, of course, this doctrine of the certainty of clear and distinct perceptions presupposes that God exists, which is precisely what these arguments are supposed to prove. Hence, the deduction of the *Meditations* would not be following the geometric order, but it would be circular and, therefore, fallacious.

The severity of this criticism for Descartes' project in the *Meditations* cannot be exaggerated; for remember that the point of the overall project is to find an absolutely certain foundation for knowledge. Recall further that this foundation is supposed to be the base for other absolutely certain truths that form a systematic body of knowledge or *scientia*. However, if the deduction by which this foundation is reached in the *Meditations* does not follow the geometric order but is circular, then the Meditator has not legitimately discovered the foundation he was seeking. Without this foundation, the possibility of an absolutely certain system of knowledge remains out of reach as well: the roots of the philosophical tree would not be firmly planted.

In Descartes' response to Arnauld, he first makes reference back to the explanation of why his reasoning is not circular made in the *Second Replies*:

> I have already given an adequate explanation of this point in my reply to the *Second Objections* ... where I made a distinction between what we in fact perceive clearly and what we remember having perceived clearly on a previous occasion. (AT VII 245–6: CSM II 171)

This distinction between what is being clearly perceived right now versus what was clearly perceived in the past is not anything new. In fact, it is reminiscent of his discussion of enumeration in the *Regulae* discussed at some length at 1.5. There Descartes explains enumeration as, among other things, a method for keeping track of each link in the chain of a long deduction, which is difficult to remember despite the performance of certain mental exercises. The point was that the necessary connection can be intuitively grasped at each and every step during the deduction, but when a deduction is quite long and the limits of human memory prevent the remembrance of each step, enumeration provides a method by which those necessary connections can be remembered. The Meditator is also concerned about the limits of human memory and how that might undermine the quest for absolutely certain knowledge.

This is precisely Descartes' point in his earlier response to this concern in the *Second Replies*:

> *Thirdly*, when I said that we can know nothing for certain until we are aware that God exists, I expressly declared that I was speaking only of knowledge of those conclusions which can be recalled when we are no longer attending to the arguments by means of which we deduced them. (AT VII 140: CSM II 100)

In this excerpt Descartes states that God's existence and, presumably, his non-deceiving nature, secures deductions that were made in the past. Interestingly enough, the Meditator had made precisely this claim in the following excerpt from the *Fifth Meditation*:

> But my nature is also such that I cannot fix my mental vision continually on the same thing so as to keep perceiving it clearly; and often the memory of a previously made judgement may come back, when I am no longer attending to the arguments which led me to make it. And so other arguments can now occur to me which might easily undermine my opinion, if I were unaware of God: and I should thus never have true and certain knowledge about anything. (AT VII 69: CSM II 48)

First, notice that the main concern is with the limitations of memory. It is impossible for a finite mind to stay fixed on the same clear and distinct deductive chain all the time. Second, since he may not remember each clear and distinct link in a deductive chain, it is possible for a preconceived opinion or perhaps some other argument to grab his attention so that he might forget or come to doubt the clarity and distinctness of that deduction. No certain knowledge could be achieved were this to happen, for then opinions would constantly change with the introduction of new arguments. Knowledge of God prevents this from happening. However, even though God's non-deceiving nature makes the memory of previous clear and distinct perceptions immune from doubt, this guarantee is not necessary for clear and distinct perceptions as they are happening.

This conclusion can be supported further by Descartes' response to Mersenne's version of the Cartesian Circle:

> It follows from this that you do not yet clearly and distinctly know that you are a thinking thing, since, on your own admission, that knowledge depends on the clear knowledge of an existing God; and this you have not yet proved in the passage where you draw the conclusion that you clearly know what you are. (AT VII 125: CSM II 89)

Here Mersenne is mainly worried about the certainty of 'I think, therefore I am' in that he does not see how it can be certain since knowledge of God is needed to guarantee its truth. But, since this argument is not made until after the conclusion 'I exist' has been reached, he does not think that the Meditator can legitimately claim to know this. Descartes responds:

> Now awareness of first principles is not normally called 'knowledge' by dialecticians. And when we become aware that we are thinking things, this is a primary notion which is not derived by means of any syllogism. When someone says 'I am thinking, therefore I am, or I exist', he does not deduce existence from thought by means of a syllogism, but recognizes it as something self-evident by a simple intuition of the mind. (AT VII 140: CSM II 100)

The main thrust of this passage is that first principles are not, strictly speaking, knowledge, and so their certainty does not require God's guarantee. This indicates that different perceptions may be immune from doubt in different ways. Recall Broughton's point discussed in 2.1 that 'I think, therefore I am' is absolutely certain, because 'my' own existence is a precondition for doubting. In other words, 'I exist' must be true in order for there to be doubt in the first place. So, this is an instance in which the activity of doubting itself makes the perception of 'I exist' absolutely certain. Notice that whether or not God exists or can be a deceiver has no role to play in establishing the absolute certainty of 'I exist'. Accordingly, 'I think, therefore I am' is known with absolute certainty even before God's existence has been proved.

Interestingly enough, Descartes uses the absolute certainty of 'I exist' as a guide for establishing the absolute certainty of other simple intuitions in this passage from the *Discourse*:

After this I considered in general what is required of a proposition in order for it to be true and certain; for since I had just found one that I knew to be such, I thought that I ought also to know what this certainty consists in. I observed that there is nothing at all in the proposition '*I am thinking, therefore I exist*' to assure me that I am speaking the truth except that I see very clearly that in order to think it is necessary to exist. So I decided that I could take it as a general rule that things we conceive very clearly and very distinctly are all true . . . (AT VI 33: CSM I 127)

Here Descartes proposes using 'I think, therefore I am' as a model of an absolutely certain truth that he clearly and distinctly perceives. This model can then be applied to other propositions in order to determine whether or not they are absolutely certain. In the *Discourse*, this model would then apply to simple mathematical truths like two plus three equals five (given the absence of the deceiving god scenario in this work). A similar claim is also made in the *Meditations* where the Meditator says that the clarity of 'I think, therefore I am' is so convincing that it makes him spontaneously declare that anything whose negation implies a 'manifest contradiction', like two plus three equals five, is true despite the fact that he is being deceived (AT VII 36: CSM II 25). But the Meditator is much more cautious here than the Descartes of the *Discourse*:

And since I have no cause to think that there is a deceiving God, and I do not yet even know for sure whether there is a God at all, any reason for doubt which depends simply on this supposition is a very slight and, so to speak, metaphysical one. But in order to remove even this slight reason for doubt, as soon as the opportunity arises I must examine whether there is a God, and, if there is, whether he can be a deceiver. For if I do not know this, it seems that I can never be quite certain about anything else. (AT VII 36: CSM II)

Here the Meditator acknowledges that the deceiving god scenario provides a very slight reason for doubt, and that anything subject to this doubt cannot be known until he discovers that God exists and cannot be a deceiver. This implies further that there may be some truths that do not depend on this, namely 'I think, therefore I am'.

This observation hints at a resolution of the Cartesian Circle. Anything that is a precondition for the deceiving god scenario is itself beyond doubt and is, therefore, absolutely certain. It has already been shown how this works in the case of 'I think, therefore I am' but presumably this is also the case with the various elements of the argument for God's existence discussed in Chapters 3 and 4. Unfortunately, this is not the place to explore this speculation any further. It should suffice for now that the Meditator or Descartes must believe that each of the premises in the arguments for God's existence found in the *Third Meditation* have the same kind of certainty as that of 'I think, therefore I am' in order to avoid the charge of circularity and maintain the validity of these arguments. Moreover, if this is true, then the Meditator can be absolutely certain of each link in the deductive chain while he is paying attention to it. But he cannot rely on his memory of the clearly and distinctly perceived (intuited) steps in that chain until he discovers that God cannot be a deceiver. Once these conclusions are reached, he can proceed with confidence in his pursuit of absolutely certain knowledge in physics.

CHAPTER 6

PHYSICS

The trunk of the philosophical tree can now grow. The metaphysical issues discussed in previous chapters now make absolutely certain knowledge in physics possible. This chapter looks at various aspects of Descartes' physics and the important ways in which it departs from the philosophy and science of his contemporaries. The second, third and fourth sections examine Descartes' points of departure from traditional, scholastic-Aristotelian science as well as the new Atomists of his day. This will then serve as a point of departure for examining Descartes' own physical theories about space and motion. But first it is important to get the flavour of the political climate for the new sciences in the seventeenth century as exemplified by the case of Galileo.

6.1 THE CONDEMNATION OF GALILEO

After moving to the United Provinces of the Netherlands in 1628, Descartes embarked on works in both metaphysics and optics. Indeed, he claims that during his first nine months there he worked on metaphysical issues and little else. But he did not think it wise to see what others thought of his metaphysics until he saw how his 'treatise on physics' was received (AT I 144: CSM K 22). This treatise on physics eventually became known as *The World, or a Treatise on Light and A Treatise on Man* and occupied Descartes' time from about 1629 to about 1633. It was in this work that Descartes hoped to develop a general theory of the universe that would replace the old Aristotelian physics taught in the universities of Europe. In this 'little treatise', as he came to call it, Descartes intended to provide the principles for explaining all physical phenomena and some of these explanations themselves. However, despite his efforts and the excitement of friends such as Mersenne and Huygens, *The World* would not see the light of day until Claude Clerselier, Descartes' literary executor, published a French version of the *Treatise on Light* in 1664, well after Descartes' death.

The reason for *The World's* suppression stems from the condemnation of Galileo by the Roman Inquisition in 1633. Galileo's problems went back to 1616 when he was forbidden to teach that the earth moved around a stationary sun. At that time, Galileo had been forbidden to hold, teach or defend this doctrine in any way, because it conflicted with a traditional interpretation of the Bible, namely the passage in Joshua 10.12 where the sun is commanded to stand still. As such, when Galileo published his famous book entitled *A Dialogue Concerning the Two Chief World Systems* in 1633, a question arose as to whether or not he had violated the earlier decree of 1616. By June 1633, Galileo was found guilty of having broken the previous decree, and he was placed under house-arrest.

Descartes interpreted all this to mean that thesis of the earth's motion around the sun had been condemned as heretical by the Catholic Church:

> Doubtless you know that Galileo was recently censured by the Inquisitors of the Faith, and that his views about the movement of the earth were condemned as heretical. I must tell you that all the things I explained in my treatise [i.e. *The World*], which included the doctrine of the movement of the earth, were so interdependent that it is enough to discover that one of them is false to know that all the arguments I was using are unsound. (AT I 285: CSM K 42)

In this letter of April 1634 to Mersenne, Descartes expresses not only his belief that Galileo's doctrine of the earth's movement was condemned but also that the principles laid out in *The World* are so dependent on that thesis that they are rendered false if the earth does not in fact move. This indicates that the earth's movement around the sun was essential to his general theory of the universe. Accordingly, this heliocentric thesis could not be removed while leaving *The World* intact. As a result, Descartes decided to submit to the Church's authority for interpreting Scripture and decided not to publish *The World*.[1]

The World was never published as a complete, self-contained work largely because no such completed work was found in the inventory of Descartes' papers after his death. Desmond Clarke points out that Descartes was interested in a wide range of topics that he hoped to integrate into a complete, self-contained work. But one might speculate that, perhaps, this integration never took place due to his decision not to publish it anyway. However, many aspects of it were later reworked and published in the essays on *Dioptics*, *Meteors* and *Geometry*, to which the *Discourse* is a preface. Other parts were also reworked and published in Parts II–IV of his *Principles of Philosophy* first published in 1644. The discussion of Descartes' physics occurring in part in 6.4 and more fully in 6.5 and 6.6 below will draw most heavily on these latter parts of the *Principles* due to the more mature nature of this work.[2] But first Descartes' break with his scholastic-Aristotelian counterparts on the issue of scientific explanation should be addressed.

6.2 FINAL CAUSES AND SUBSTANTIAL FORMS

Questions that begin with 'why' such as 'Why do spiders build webs?', 'Why is my television missing?' and 'Why do you want to take Introduction to Philosophy?' are usually answered with 'because . . .' What follows the 'because' is a causal story or explanation of the phenomenon in question. However, not all 'because' responses are the same. For example, someone may want to take Introduction to Philosophy, *because* she wants to achieve the goal of satisfying a General Education requirement; or my television is missing, *because* a tornado blew through my house and flung it twenty miles away. These are two very different kinds of causal story or explanation commonly used to account for why things happen as they do. The former explanation is based on the student's goal, while the latter is based on the source of my television's movement. Accordingly, not all explanations invoke the same causal principles. In fact, the Scholastics, based on their understanding of Aristotle, claimed that there were four such principles or causes: final, efficient, formal and material.

The final cause will be discussed first. The example provided above shows how the goal of satisfying a General Education requirement explains why this student is taking Introduction to Philosophy. According to Aristotle, this kind of cause is also operable in the non-human, natural world. For example, plants send their roots down and not up for the sake of achieving the goal of providing themselves with nutrition. Second, the efficient cause is generally unpacked as a cause of physical motion. The explanation of why my television is missing is based on the tornado as the efficient cause of my television's movement from my living room to some place twenty miles away. For present purposes it is also important to notice that the tornado did not move my television for the sake of some end or goal but it did so 'blindly' without any end in sight. Given its current force (or motion for Descartes), its contact with a non-moving object of a given weight and the laws of nature, the television was moved that distance, no more and no less, by the tornado. Hence, final causes are based on goals while efficient causes are, when viewed in isolation, purposeless.

Although these two kinds of causes appear, in some sense, to be opposite from each other, they work together in the formal cause and its relation to the material cause. The material cause is the 'stuff' out of which something is made, whereas the formal cause is the principle organizing that 'stuff' or matter in a certain way. For example, a statue of a horse can be made out of clay, i.e. its matter, and what makes it the statue of a horse instead of a bird, turtle, truck or something else is the way in which that clay has been organized, i.e. its form. For Aristotle, and the Scholastics after him, the same form-matter framework is at work in the non-human, natural world. All physical things are fundamentally made out of the same matter but what differentiates them from one another are their various forms. Hence, a dog and a tree are both made out of some fundamental matter or stuff but what makes one a dog and the other a tree is the form of that stuff. If that matter is organized in one way, then it is a dog. If it is organized in another way, then it is a tree. If organized in some third way, then it is a spider, and so on.

Notice that the form determines what something is, because everything is made out of matter but only the organization of that matter determines whether it is a dog, tree or spider kind of thing. This points towards a further distinction among kinds of forms. Some forms are 'substantial' in that they determine the essence, nature or substance of a thing. For instance, the form of dog is a substantial form, because it is the principle by which matter is organized to be a dog kind of thing. Substantial forms, then, cannot change in a thing without completely changing the thing's essence and making it some other kind of thing. However, accidental forms can change without any effect on something's essence. For instance, a tree can have leaves at one time of year but not at another. That tree has several forms of 'being leafed' during the spring and summer months but not during the winter. Losing its leaves does not change or affect the essence of a tree – it is still a tree, with or without leaves – and so 'being leafed' is a form accidental to the essence or substance of a tree.

Now, another important feature of matter and form is their relation of act and potency. Broadly speaking, potency is found in the material side of things. Returning to the clay, a hunk of clay is potentially a statue, a vase, a bowl, a coffee cup, etc. But it is not actually any of these things until it takes on the form of a horse, vase or coffee cup. Accordingly, the material cause is the potency in something for taking on a certain form (in this case, the clay), whereas the formal cause is the active principle by which that potency becomes actual (in this case, the organization of the clay into a coffee cup). But how does a hunk of clay become a coffee cup? Well, surely this is the result of some artisan, who sets the goal of making a coffee cup and then moves the clay around in such a way as to form a coffee cup. Hence, a complete explanation of the coffee cup's existence involves not just the formal and material causes but also the final and efficient causes as well.

Again, for Aristotle and the Scholastics, the same is true in the natural world. The substantial form (i.e. formal cause) actualizes the potential in matter (i.e. material cause) for being some kind of thing. Since the form determines the being of the thing, it was thought to establish the end for the sake of which the rest of the being is organized, i.e. its final cause. Indeed, in *On the Principles of Nature*, Thomas Aquinas considers the final cause to be the 'cause of causes' in that it is what gets everything else going. For example, the substantial form of 'dogness' actualizes this potential in matter by establishing the goal of being a dog. The matter is then 'moved around' (so to speak) or efficiently caused to take on a certain organization in order to achieve this goal. Notice that all four causes are at work here. The material cause is just the potency for being a dog and the formal cause actualizes this potency through the establishment of this end (final cause) and the execution of the steps (efficient cause) required for achieving that end. Nevertheless, the final cause's status as the cause of causes makes it the ultimate explanatory principle for why something is the way it is such that everything about that thing, e.g. a dog, is ultimately explained by the goal of being a dog. Some of the implications of this for the scholastic-Aristotelian theory of scientific explanation and Descartes' rejections of them are discussed in the next section.

6.3 THE REJECTION OF FINAL CAUSES

The cornerstone of the traditional scholastic-Aristotelian theory of scientific explanation is the doctrine of final causes, for without the 'cause of causes' the doctrine of matter and form central to all scholastic metaphysics and physics cannot even get off the ground. Moreover, once the scholastic apparatus has collapsed, the field is left wide open for some rival theory of scientific explanation to take its place. This section examines Descartes' rejection of final causes, while the next two discuss both Descartes' new theory and some of its rivals.

Broadly speaking, Descartes' rejection of the use of final causes in explanations of physical phenomena is twofold. The first is really a set of concerns derived from their weakness as explanatory principles. In May 1643 Descartes published an open letter in response to some harsh criticisms about his philosophy published by Gisbertus Voetius, rector of the University of Utrecht, and his accomplice Martin Schook at the University of Leiden:

> The ordinary philosophy which is taught in the schools and universities is by contrast merely a collection of opinions that are for the most part doubtful, as is shown by the continual debates in which they are thrown back and forth. They are quite useless, moreover, as long experience has shown to us; for no one has ever succeeded in deriving any practical benefit from 'prime matter', 'substantial forms', 'occult qualities' and the like. (AT VIIIB 26: CSM K 221)

Although this passage does not explicitly call out final causes for criticism, the reference to 'substantial forms', which bestow a final cause on a thing, amounts to a criticism of final causation as well. In this passage, Descartes makes two important criticisms of 'substantial forms' and their concomitant final causes. The first is that opinions about them are not certain but doubtful. This makes them useless as principles of explanation because the explanations based on such doubtful principles would themselves be doubtful. Accordingly, no certain scientific knowledge or *scientia* can be derived from them. This unintelligibility is characterized in the following way in the *Fourth Meditation*:

> I consider the customary search for final causes to be totally useless in physics; there is considerable rashness in thinking

myself capable of investigating the purposes of God. (AT VII 55: CSM II 39)

Here the obscure nature of final causes is a result of the Meditator's mental limitations in trying to investigate God's purposes. The French version of *Principles* I.28 later enjoins the reader to 'banish from our philosophy the search for final causes' in favour of the efficient causes of created things (AT VIIIA 15: CSM I 202). Hence, their unintelligible nature as God's purposes is enough to ignore final causes altogether when conducting scientific enquiry and replacing them with efficient causal explanations.

The second criticism expressed in the letter to Voetius points out that explanations derived from these principles have not yielded any beneficial results. This claim points to the uninformative nature of final causal explanations. For example, the fact that swallows build nests was explained by the fact that this activity is directed towards achieving the goal of being a swallow. Accordingly, an answer to the question 'Why do swallows build nests?' would be something like 'Because it is the nature or essence of a swallow to be disposed for nest-building.' Although this explanation is true, it is uninformative. This would be like saying Ambien puts people to sleep because it has the power for putting people to sleep. This does not tell us anything about how this power works and, therefore, such explanations cannot result in any new knowledge.

Descartes, however, seeks to replace obscure and uninformative final causal explanations with efficient causal explanations based on the configuration and motion of bodily parts, because the principle that bodies are made up of parts in motion 'is visible to the naked eye in many cases and can be proved by countless reasons in others' (AT II 200: CSM K 107). Hence, Descartes believes that these kinds of efficient causal explanations are clearer and more intelligible than their final causal counterparts. Accordingly, unlike final causal explanations based on substantial forms, etc., these efficient causal explanations based on the configuration and motion of parts can yield clear and certain explanations from which new knowledge and real benefits might be attained.

The second main criticism of final causes is that they constitute an illicit ascription of mental properties to entirely physical, non-mental things. Descartes is quite explicit about this in the following passage from the *Sixth Replies*:

> But what makes it especially clear that my idea of gravity was taken largely from the idea I had of the mind is the fact that I thought that gravity carried bodies toward the centre of the earth as if it had some knowledge of the centre within itself. For this surely could not happen without knowledge, and there can be no knowledge except in a mind. Nevertheless, I continued to apply to gravity various other attributes which cannot be understood to apply to a mind in this way – for example its being divisible, measurable and so on. (AT VII 442: CSM II 298)

The Scholastics, following Aristotle, understood gravity to be a quality existing ultimately for the sake of being a bodily kind of thing. This quality is just a tendency for moving towards its natural place, viz. the centre of the earth. Accordingly, bodies fall downward when unimpeded by external forces in order to achieve their goal of reaching the centre of the earth. In this passage, Descartes argues that this implies that any body, including inanimate ones like stones, must have knowledge of the earth's centre itself. For instance, a stone must know what the centre of the earth is and where it is in order to take the steps necessary for achieving its goal of reaching it. But knowledge is found only in minds. Hence, to ascribe a purpose to an entirely physical, non-mental thing is to implicitly and mistakenly ascribe a mental property to something without a mind.[3] Indeed, Descartes goes on to argue that the scholastic idea of body is the result of confusing the idea of the mind with the idea of the body (AT VII 442–3: CSM II 298). Therefore, this ascription of final causes in physics is an illicit projection of the idea of the human mind onto completely physical, non-mental things. Accordingly, it is a mistake to use final causes as explanatory principles in physics.

This rejection of final causes has several consequences. First, the replacement of final causal explanations with efficient causal ones indicates a reverse in the accepted explanatory order. Recall that, on the scholastic account, the final cause or goal of being that kind of thing was the cause that explains why that thing is organized as it is with certain dispositions. For example, a disposition for flight was thought to be the cause that explains why birds are organized so as to have wings. But Descartes believes that the explanatory order should go in the other direction: it is the organization of matter into a bird with wings that explains the fact that birds can fly. Accordingly, for Descartes, dispositions for certain kinds of activity are not the causes of material organization but rather they are the effects of that organization. The second consequence is that the rejection of final causal principles leaves the field wide open for some other set of explanatory principles to take its place. The next section addresses Descartes' rejection of one of these competing theories in favour of his own.

6.4 THE REJECTION OF ATOMISM

The replacement of final causal with efficient causal explanations marks perhaps the fundamental shift from the old, traditional science to the new, modern science that has been so successful even into the present day. This shift to efficient causes also marks a shift in world view. In the scholastic tradition, the world is alive and full of God's purposes, while in modern science, the world is a machine that needs to be figured out. Broadly speaking, this mechanistic world view maintains that the physical universe is ultimately made up of microscopic bodies in motion. These minuscule bodies in motion were then the efficient causal explanatory principles that took the place of the now rejected final causes. Atomism was one of these mechanistic theories.

Atomism goes back to the ancient Greek philosophers Democritus and Leucippus. This ancient doctrine, though not entirely forgotten, received renewed interest in the seventeenth century due to the rediscovery and translation from Greek into Latin of some of these ancient texts. Pierre Gassendi, the author of the *Fifth Objections*, was one of the more prominent Atomists of his time, who maintained that everything was composed of indivisible atoms moving around in a void. Accordingly, everything either is an atom or is composed of atoms bearing certain relationships to one another. It is this doctrine of indivisible atoms and an empty space or void that distinguished Atomism from other theories that were also based on the motion of microscopic bodies. Therefore, it is these two doctrines that Descartes attacks in distinguishing his own physics from theirs.

Descartes rejects the doctrine that atoms are indivisible bodies at *Principles* II.20:

> For if there were any atoms, then no matter how small we imagined them to be, they would necessarily have to be extended; and hence we could in our thought divide each of them into two or more smaller parts, and hence recognize their divisibility. (AT VIIIA 51: CSM I 231)

So, the notion of an indivisible body is a contradiction in terms, because extension is divisible by its very nature and, therefore, so long as something is an extended thing it can be divided into two or more smaller parts. This section of the *Principles* continues on to address a possible objection:

> Even if we imagine that God has chosen to bring it about that some particle of matter is incapable of being divided into smaller particles, it will still not be correct, strictly speaking, to call this particle indivisible.

Here the objection is that maybe God has made some extended things so that they could never actually be divided. But, Descartes responds, this particle would not, strictly speaking, be indivisible. He continues:

> For, by making it indivisible by any of his creatures, God certainly could not thereby take away his own power of dividing it . . . Hence, strictly speaking, the particle will remain divisible, since it is divisible by its very nature. (AT VIIIA 51–2: CSM I 231–2)

Thus, extension is potentially divisible into infinity, because it is always possible for God to divide some particle of matter, however small, into two or more even smaller parts (see letter to Gibeuf dated 1642 at AT III 477: CSM K 202–3). Therefore, the existence of atoms is impossible, because it is precisely the notion of an indivisible extended thing, which is a contradiction in terms.

The doctrine of a void, vacuum or empty space is another of Descartes' Atomistic targets. In a 1638 letter to Mersenne, Descartes claims that 'it is, I think, just as impossible that a space should be empty as that a mountain should be without a valley' (AT II 440: CSM K 129). This indicates that just as the conception of a mountain without a valley is unintelligible, so also is the conception of an empty space, for it is the notion of a non-extended body. Further elaboration is found at *Principles* II.18 where Descartes uses the example of the extension inside a concave vessel to make the same point (see AT VIIIA 50: CSM I 230–1). A full wine bottle will make a nice example. After the wine has been drunk, it is common to say that the bottle is empty. But in the strict philosophical sense, this cannot be true, for the bottle's sides are a certain distance from each other and, since distance is a mode of extension, it follows that there is extended substance present inside the bottle. Indeed, everyone would agree that air is the extended substance that replaced the wine inside the bottle. But if God were to annihilate all the extension within that bottle, then there would be nothing capable of having a mode of distance in it, and therefore there would be no distance between its sides. As a result, the sides of the wine bottle would touch. The point is that the notion of an empty space is, strictly speaking, a contradiction in terms, because it is the notion of an extended thing that is not extended. Therefore, this facet of Atomism should be rejected as well.

In the end, Descartes has shown that the fundamental principles of Atomism are themselves self-contradictory, and therefore Atomism must be false. The rejection of the possibility of a void or vacuum leaves open an account of the 'place' in which those particular bodies move around. The rejection of the vacuum leaves two remaining plausible theories of space and place. The first theory is that there are two different kinds of extension. One would be the impenetrable extension that constitutes bodies while the other would be the penetrable extension constituting the space in which those bodies reside. The second theory is that the physical universe is a *plenum* of individual bodies wherein the place of any body is determined by its relation to other bodies instead of by some coordinates within the container space constituted by a penetrable kind of extension. As will be seen in the next section, Descartes embraces the latter, *plenum*, option while rejecting the former, container space, option.

6.5 SPACE AND PLACE

Any physics requires some general account of space and the bodies occupying various places within it. Descartes makes the following claim about space or 'internal place' at *Principles* II.10:

> There is no real distinction between space, or internal place, and the corporeal substance contained in it; the only difference lies in the way in which we are accustomed to conceive of them. For in reality the extension in length, breadth and depth which constitutes a space is exactly the same as that which constitutes a body. (AT VIIIA 45: CSM I 227)

In this passage, Descartes is maintaining that a particular body and the space that it is said to occupy are 'exactly the same'. This is clarified in the following section:

> It is easy for us to recognize that the extension constituting the nature of a body is exactly the same as that constituting the nature of space. There is no more difference between them than there is between the nature of a genus or species and the nature of an individual. (AT VIIIA 46: CSM I 227)

This passage from *Principles* II.11 indicates that the extension that constitutes a particular body is exactly the same as the extension constituting the space that body is said to occupy. Jorge Secada and others understand this to mean that extension itself is continuous space while a body is merely a modified part of that space such that space just is body in general.[4] However, these passages are better understood in light of Descartes' rejection of the notion of space as a container in which particular bodies reside. According to this theory, space contains bodies such that God could annihilate all bodies, while the empty container space in which they resided would continue to exist. This means that the extension constituting space and that constituting the body said to occupy that space are really distinct from one another, because the container space can exist without the body in it. Hence, Descartes' claim at *Principles* II.10 quoted above is an explicit rejection of this view.

This view can also be contrasted with the Aristotelian doctrine that space is just a *plenum* or collection of particular bodies. On this account, a body's place is determined by its relation to other bodies in the *plenum* as opposed to some coordinate within a container space. The Aristotelian account is based on the claim that two things with spatial dimensions (i.e. length, breadth and depth) cannot simultaneously occupy one place. This means that it is impossible for two extended things to occupy the same place as would have to be the case if a particular body were to occupy the extended space within this container. So, for Aristotle as for Descartes, all extension is of the impenetrable kind. However, some contemporaries of Descartes wanted to maintain a container notion of space and tried to avoid this concern by positing two kinds of extension. One kind is material and requires space but cannot exist in the same place with another material quantity – this is the impenetrable extension of particular bodies. The other kind is penetrable and permits a body to coexist with it, which is the extension of space. This latter kind of extension came to be called 'imaginary space', which was conceived as the container in which bodies reside and was, therefore, defined as a capacity for receiving bodies endowed with material or impenetrable extension or quantity.[5]

Descartes' claim in the above-quoted passages that the extension of bodies and that of space are exactly the same is a direct denial of the existence of imaginary space or any other kind of extension besides that constituting particular bodies. What follows the passage from *Principles* II.10 cited above will help shed light on the way in which the extension of body and space are 'exactly the same':

> The difference arises as follows: in the case of a body, we regard the extension as something particular, and thus think of it as changing whenever there is a new body, but in the case of a space, we attribute to the extension only a generic unity, so that when a new body comes to occupy the space, the extension of the space is reckoned not to change but to remain one and the same, so long as it retains the same size and shape and keeps the same position relative to certain external bodies which we use to determine the space in question. (AT VIIIA 45: CSM I 227)

Contrary to the notion of imaginary space, Descartes claims at both *Principles* II.10 and 11 that the extension of body and that of space are the same. But section 10 states that they differ in that the extension of a body is particular whereas the extension of space is generic. Furthermore, section 11 makes the claim that there is no more difference between them than between a genus or species and the nature of an individual. Recall from 3.4 that for Descartes universals such as genera and species are modes of thinking derived from the consideration of what particular things have in common, i.e. by abstraction. So generic extension is merely a mode of thinking or idea abstracted from the ideas of particular extended things.

Two lessons can be drawn from these considerations. First, extension by its very nature is impenetrable and, therefore, no two extended things can exist in the same place at the same time. This then eliminates the possibility of penetrable extension or imaginary space since impenetrable extension would then be impossible. Second, space is just an abstraction from the perception of particular extended things. Accordingly, what is called 'space' is just an idea in the mind and does not exist separately from particular extended things. This then implies that the physical universe is a *plenum* of particular bodies, existing side by side without an empty space or imaginary space between them. Further reflection on Descartes' conception of place will help shed further light on his doctrine of a *plenum*.

Descartes describes external place at *Principles* II.13 as being determined by a body's relative position to the bodies surrounding it:

> The terms 'place' and 'space', then, do not signify anything different from the body which is said to be in a place; they merely refer to its size, shape, and position relative to other bodies. To determine the position, we have to look at various other bodies which we regard as immobile. (AT VIIIA 47: CSM I 228)

In this passage, Descartes defines a body's place not by its coordinates in a container space but in relation to the other bodies surrounding it. An example should help illustrate Descartes' point. Books in a bookcase are both adjacent to other books and contained on a bookshelf. Those endorsing a container space see place and space as like the bookshelf and the books to be like particular bodies occupying that place. Accordingly, the place of a particular body would be its coordinates within that container just as a particular book's place would be determined by its coordinates in the bookcase, e.g. third shelf from the top and 2 feet from the right. But Descartes' *plenum* theory does not recognize the existence of the metaphorical 'bookcase' of the container or imaginary space theory. Instead, a particular body's location would be determined by its relation to other bodies just as a particular book's place can be determined by its relation to other books, e.g. it's the one between *War and Peace* and *Harry Potter and the Half-Blood Prince*.

Accordingly, since there is no imaginary space to constitute a place for Descartes, the particular body said to 'occupy' that place and its relation to the particular bodies surrounding it are what constitute that place. This raises an interesting issue for Descartes, which is raised in the following excerpt from *Principles* II.12:

> There is, however, a difference in the way in which we conceive of space and corporeal substance. For if a stone is removed from the space or place where it is, we think that its extension has also been removed from the place, since we regard the extension as something particular and inseparable from the stone. But, at the same time we think that the extension of the place where the stone used to be remains, and is the same as before, although the place is now

occupied by wood or water or air or some other body . . . (AT VIIIA 46: CSM I 228)

When a stone is removed from a place, we understand that the extension of that stone goes with it to its new location. But despite this understanding, we still think that the extension of the place where the stone used to be remains even though some other body occupies that place. Descartes goes on to say:

> For we are now considering extension as something general, which is thought of as being the same, whether it is the extension of a stone or of wood or of water or air or of any other body . . . provided only that it has the same size and shape, and keeps the same position relative to the external bodies that determine the space in question. (AT VIIIA 46–7: CSM I 228)

An example will help to illustrate Descartes' point. Let us return to the wine bottle. The bottle's internal place is constituted by the wine contained in it. Once the wine is finished, the bottle's internal place is now constituted by another part of extension, viz. the quantity of air now occupying it. Notice that the extension of the wine and that of the air are different, and so the wine bottle's internal place was constituted by two different bits of extension at two different times. So, strictly speaking, the bottle has two internal places: one constituted by the wine and the other constituted by air. But since these two parts of extension have the same shape, size and position relative to the bottle, which is the body surrounding it, it is said that air is now in the place of the wine. On this account, place is considered in general, regardless of whatever particular piece of extension bears the requisite relation to the bottle. Hence, space and therefore place, are mere abstractions existing in the mind. But a particular place in the world can be constituted first by one particular extended thing and then by another.

6.6 THE NATURE OF MOTION

The most fundamental element of Descartes' physics is motion, for it is motion that accounts for 'all the variety in matter, all the diversity of its forms' (AT VIIIA 52: CSM I 232. See also AT XI 34: CSM I 91). He then goes on to distinguish 'motion' in the ordinary sense of the term from 'motion' in the strict sense. The ordinary sense of the term is addressed in the following passage from *Principles* II.24: 'Motion, in the ordinary sense of the term, is simply *the action by which a body travels from one place to another*' (AT VIIIA 53: CSM I 233). Two aspects of this ordinary sense of 'motion' stand out. First, the scholastic nature of this sense of the term is marked when 'motion' is being defined as an 'action'. Accordingly, this action is defined as merely the actualization of a potential or a disposition for motion, which is uninformative. Moreover, as Descartes notes at the end of this section, rest would then be defined as the cessation of this action, i.e. as an unactualized potential for travelling from place to place, which is again uninformative.

Second, motion occurs when 'a body travels from one place to another'. This reliance on place then gives rise to a relative notion of motion such that the same thing can be considered in motion or at rest depending on one's perspective. Descartes goes on to give the following example:

> For example, a man sitting on board a ship which is leaving part considers himself to be moving relative to the shore which he regards as fixed; but he does not think of himself as moving relative to the ship, since his position is unchanged relative to its parts. (AT VIIIA 53: CSM I 233)

The point of this example is that the man is both in motion and not in motion or at rest. He is at motion relative to the shore since he is travelling out of that place and into another in this respect. But he is not in motion relative to the ship since he is sitting and is not travelling from one place on the ship to another. However, Descartes concludes this section by noting that the man is more properly said to be at rest since he does not have any sensory awareness of this action in himself. One can extrapolate from this that it is, therefore, the ship that is properly said to be in motion. This last point provides a clue as to how Descartes' more strict account of motion is supposed to avoid this relative aspect of the ordinary sense.

Descartes discusses 'motion' in the strict sense in the following passage from *Principles* II.25:

> If, on the other hand, we consider what should be understood by *motion*, not in common usage but in accordance with the truth of the matter, and if our aim is to assign a determinate nature to it, we may say that *motion is the transfer of one piece of matter, or one*

> *body, from the vicinity of the other bodies which are in immediate contact with it, and which are regarded as being at rest, to the vicinity of other bodies.* (AT VIIIA 53: CSM I 233)

Notice that Descartes' definition of motion is partially based on a body's relation to the other bodies immediately in contact with it (i.e. its external place). Motion, then, is relative to a set of bodies that are considered at rest such that a particular body travels from one set of surrounding bodies with which it is in immediate contact to another set of surrounding bodies with which it comes into contact. Hence, returning to the example of a man on a ship, the man is, strictly speaking, at rest because he continues to be in immediate contact with the bodies surrounding him, while the ship is in motion because it is travelling from one set of surrounding bodies to another. On Descartes' account, motion is no longer relative in the sense that the man is no longer both moving and at rest – he is only at rest given his relation to the bodies *immediately surrounding him and regarded as being at rest*.

Descartes, however, expands on his account of motion at *Principles* II.29 where the significance of the surrounding bodies being 'regarded as being at rest' becomes evident:

> For transfer is in itself a reciprocal process: we cannot understand that a body AB is transferred from the vicinity of a body CD without simultaneously understanding that CD is transferred from the vicinity of AB. Exactly the same force and action is needed on both sides. So if we wished to characterize motion strictly in terms of its own nature, without reference to anything else, then in the case of two contiguous bodies being transferred in opposite directions, and thus separate, we should say that there was just as much motion in the one body as in the other. (AT VIIIA 55–6: CSM I 235)

The point here is that one body can be regarded as being in motion only if the other bodies surrounding it with which it is in contact are regarded as being at rest. But, as Descartes notes here, two bodies in immediate contact with one another can both be regarded as in motion since each is being transferred from the vicinity of the other. So, Descartes is willing to admit that motion is still, in some sense, relative in that it depends on one's perspective, viz. it depends on which bodies are 'regarded' as being at rest. This, however, does not undermine the clear distinction between motion and rest that Descartes wished to draw. For motion, when taken absolutely, is just two bodies separating themselves in opposite directions, and therefore they are both regarded as being in motion and not at rest.[6]

6.7 THE LAWS OF MOTION

Yet although one body may be regarded as at rest at one moment but in motion at another, this does not mean that the quantity of motion in the universe has been increased. Rather the immutability of God's nature implies that the quantity of motion in the universe must not change, and so no quantity of motion is ever added to or subtracted from the universe, as stated at *Principles* II.36.[7] Instead, quantities of motion are merely passed from one body to another in accordance with certain general laws of motion established by God at creation. Descartes argues in his early, unpublished work, *The World*, that God kept various bodies in motion, at different rates of speed, and in different directions, and that the laws God established for their movement were so marvellous that 'even if we suppose he creates nothing beyond what I have mentioned and sets up no order or proportion within it but composes from it a chaos . . . the laws of nature are sufficient to cause the parts of this chaos to disentangle themselves and arrange themselves in such good order that they will have the form of a quite perfect world' (AT XI 34–5: CSM I 91). Hence, the system of motion's laws is just the order God has established in the physical universe.

It is then easy to see how Descartes' first law of motion is derived from God's immutability: 'each and every thing, in so far as it can, always continues in the same state; and thus what is once in motion always continues to move' (AT VIIIA 62: CSM I 240). The point is that God's will preserves a thing's quantity of motion so long as it does not come into contact with some other thing with which it might transfer some mode of motion. So a body moving at a certain rate of speed will continue to move at that speed indefinitely unless it comes into contact with another body. This is, of course, only an ideal since the physical world is just a *plenum* of particular bodies, and therefore a body in motion must always come into contact with some other body.

The second law of motion is that 'all motion is in itself rectilinear; and hence any body moving in a circle always tends to move away from the centre of the circle which it describes' (AT VIIIA 63–4:

CSM I 241–2). This is also justified by God's immutability and simplicity in that he will preserve a quantity of motion in the exact form in which it is occurring, i.e. in the same direction, until some created thing comes along to change it. The principle expressed here is that any body considered all by itself tends to move in a straight line unless it collides with another body, which deflects it. Notice that this is a thesis about any body left all by itself, and so only lone bodies will continue to move in a straight line. But again, since the physical world is a *plenum* for Descartes, bodies are not really all by themselves, but they are constantly colliding with one another.

This leads to Descartes' famous doctrine of vortices explicitly stated at *Principles* II.33. In this context, a vortex is a whirling set of particular bodies. Descartes believes that this must follow from the thesis that the physical universe is a *plenum* of bodies, for a moving body must displace another body in the *plenum* and replace it in order to constitute that place (see 6.4). Accordingly, one moving body must collide with and replace another body, which, in turn, is set in motion and collides with another body, replacing it and so on. But at the end of this series of collisions and replacements, the last body moved must then collide with and replace the first body in the sequence. To illustrate: suppose that body A collides with and replaces body B, B replaces C, C replaces D, and then D replaces A. For Descartes, the physical universe is made up of a set of such vortices (see AT VIIIA 58–9: CSM I 237–8).

The third general law of motion is as follows:

> If a body collides with another body that is stronger than itself, it loses none of its motion; but if it collides with a weaker body, it loses a quantity of motion equal to that which is imparts to the other body. (AT VIIIA 65: CSM I 242)

This is the law governing what Daniel Garber calls a 'contest' principle of impact. When two bodies come into contact there is a contest between them that determines which body moves and in what direction. The outcome of this contest is determined by their respective quantities of motion and ability to resist other bodies.[8] The first part concerning deflection is based on the distinction between a body's quantity of motion and its 'determination', i.e. its direction. Descartes argues at *Principles* II.41 (in accordance with the previous laws) that God will conserve the same motion and direction in a body unless it comes into contact with some other body that can change one or the other. Accordingly, when a moving body comes into contact with a stronger or more resistant body, the former loses the contest. It does not transfer a mode of motion to the stronger body but maintains its quantity of motion while changing direction. For example, when someone throws a tennis ball against the wall, no mode of motion is transferred to the wall since the wall does not move. Yet, the tennis ball's direction is no longer towards the wall but away from it. Hence, the wall wins the contest because its ability to resist was greater than the tennis ball's ability to move in that direction.[9]

The second part of this law states that when a moving body comes into contact with a weaker body, then it loses the same amount of motion as was transferred to the weaker body. Hence, the moving body wins the contest to the extent that it continues to move. However, the continuation of motion is decreased in equal proportion as the weaker body is set in motion. Suppose, for the sake of illustration, a baseball is thrown at a stationary soda bottle. The baseball would win the contest because its ability to move in that direction is greater than the bottle's ability to resist it, and therefore the bottle would be set in motion. Accordingly, the bottle's motion does not add any new motion to the world but has instead been transferred to it from the baseball, and so the bottle's increase in motion is offset by the baseball's loss of motion. Hence, the quantity of motion gained by the bottle is equal to the quantity of motion lost by the baseball.

This concludes the brief account of Descartes' physics of bodies in motion, which he sums up nicely at *Principles* III.46:

> From what has already been said we have established that all the bodies in the universe are composed of one and the same matter, which is divisible into indefinitely many parts, and is in fact divided into a large number of parts which move in different directions and have a sort of circular motion; moreover, the same quantity of motion is always preserved in the universe. (AT VIIIA 100: CSM I 256)

With Descartes' mechanical picture of the physical universe and its laws in hand, it is time to move on to explain the senses in which Descartes maintained the earth was both in motion and at rest.

6.8 THE EARTH'S MOTION

Recall from 6.1 that the issue as to whether the earth was in motion or at rest was a hot topic at Descartes' time. Traditionally the Church maintained that the earth was at rest, and that the sun, stars and planets revolved around it. However, other, more modern natural philosophers, like Galileo, maintained that the earth moved, and that it was the earth's motion that gave the appearance that the stars, etc. moved around it. Although Descartes decided not to publicly display his own position that the earth is in motion in the 1630s, he found a way to split the difference by the time the *Principles* was published in 1644 by arguing that the earth is in motion in one sense but at rest in another.

Recall from 6.6 that, strictly speaking, something is in motion if it is transferred from the vicinity of the bodies immediately surrounding it that are considered at rest to some other set of bodies. The example of a man on a ship was used to illustrate Descartes' point. A man sitting on a ship is not in motion relative to the ship, since he is not being transferred from the vicinity of the bodies immediately surrounding him. But the ship is, strictly speaking, in motion precisely because it is being transferred from the bodies immediately surrounding it, i.e. the dock, land, water particles, to another. So, in this scenario, the man is, strictly speaking, at rest, while the ship is, strictly speaking, in motion. However, the man can be *said* to be in motion in an ordinary or loose sense of 'motion' in that he is being carried along with the ship and so he is in motion relative to the shore. According to Descartes, the earth is both at rest and in motion in the same way as the man on the ship.

Making this analogy requires the further recollection that Descartes rejects the doctrine of a vacuum or empty space. Accordingly, the earth does not exist in either an empty or imaginary space but is a member of the *plenum* of bodies comprising the universe. The 'heavens' then are just the *plena* of bodies immediately surrounding the earth, which moves in a vortex around the sun, carrying the earth along with it. Now, just like the man on the ship, the earth is, strictly speaking, not in motion but at rest. This is because the earth, like the man, is not being transferred from the vicinity of the bodies immediately surrounding it. But it is being carried along by something else that is in motion. Here the heavens act as the 'ship' of the earth, carrying it around the sun, and so, like the ship, the heavens are, strictly speaking, in motion due to their transference relative to the bodies immediately surrounding them and considered at rest. But just as the man on the ship can, in a loose or ordinary sense of the word, be considered in motion relative to the shore, so the earth can also be loosely considered in motion relative to other heavenly bodies. However, Descartes thinks that considering the earth to be in motion in this ordinary sense is a mistake:

> But if we construe 'motion' in accordance with ordinary usage, then all the other planets, and even the sun and fixed stars should be said to move; but the same cannot without great awkwardness be said of the Earth. For the common practice is to determine the position of the stars from certain sites on the Earth that are regarded as being immobile; the stars are deemed to move in so far as they pass these fixed spots. This is convenient for practical purposes, and so is quite reasonable. (AT VIIIA 91: CSM I 252)

So, the Descartes of 1644 is still reluctant to officially ascribe any real motion to the earth in accordance with Church doctrine.

CHAPTER 7

HUMAN NATURE

The branches of physiology and morals are supposed to grow from the trunk of physics in Descartes' tree of philosophy. But before these branches can be examined, it is important to understand Descartes' theory of human nature occurring at the intersection between metaphysics and the physics of mechanism (since physiology and morals pertain only to living human beings composed of both mind and body). The first two sections examine Descartes' arguments for the real distinction between mind and body while the next five examine how they are supposed to be united to form one whole human being. The conclusion is eventually reached that mind and body are actually united in a human being but only potentially separate. The final section then looks at various remarks made by Descartes on human life and death, thereby laying the groundwork for the discussions of physiology and morals in Chapter 8.

7.1 THE CONCEPTUAL ARGUMENT

The Meditator's first argument for the real distinction of mind and body occurs in the following excerpt from the *Sixth Meditation*:

> [O]n the one hand I have a clear and distinct idea of myself, in so far as I am simply a thinking, non-extended thing, and on the other hand I have a distinct idea of body, in so far as this is simply an extended, non-thinking thing. And accordingly, it is certain that I am really distinct from my body, and can exist without it. (AT VII 78: CSM II 54)

The gist of the argument is really quite simple. Here the Meditator is claiming to have a clear and distinct idea of the 'I' or mind all by itself without the body as well as a clear and distinct idea of his body all by itself without the 'I' or mind. This is just an application of the criterion for a real distinction discussed in 3.1. The Meditator is here claiming that he can exclude all that pertains to the body from his intellectual perception of the mind, and all that pertains to the mind can be excluded from his intellectual perception of the body. Accordingly, he understands each as depending only on God's power and, therefore, capable of existing all by itself. Hence, mind and body are two really distinct substances.

Another important feature of this argument is the Meditator's reliance on the doctrine of clear and distinct ideas. First, the Meditator seems to be claiming an intuitive grasp of these two natures as being mutually exclusive. Second, recall from Chapter 5 that the truth of all clear and distinct perceptions is guaranteed by the facts that God exists and cannot be a deceiver. So, the Meditator's claim that his perception of the respective natures of mind and body are clear and distinct means that he cannot be mistaken about them. This then secures the deduction from these two ideas of mind and body to the conclusion that each can exist without the other. Therefore, the argument works from within Descartes' epistemological framework. But if this epistemological foundation turns out to be faulty, then all bets are off.

Indeed, without his epistemological foundation the Meditator is making mere bald assertions about how he perceives mind and body. A question then arises about whether or not he (or anyone) really has a 'clear' understanding of the mind without a body or a body without a mind. This latter case is easy to put to rest due to the fact that many bodies do in fact exist without a mind, e.g. stones. However, examples of minds existing without bodies are not so easily found. Some even go so far as to claim that they cannot conceive of a mind without a body, i.e. without a brain. They would argue that a brain is necessary for thinking and, therefore, minds just are bodies or extended things. If this were true, then it would be impossible for a thinking thing to exist all by itself without extension. Hence, it would then be impossible for the mind to survive the death of the body. So, in the end, the certainty of this argument stands or falls with the viability of his epistemological foundation. Since just about everyone but Descartes rejects God's non-deceiving nature as a foundation for knowledge, many find this argument very unconvincing.

7.2 THE DIVISIBILITY/INDIVISIBILITY ARGUMENT

The argument just examined is formulated in a different way later in the *Sixth Meditation*:

> [T]here is a great difference between the mind and the body, inasmuch as the body is by its very nature always divisible, while the mind is utterly indivisible. For when I consider the mind, or myself in so far as I am merely a thinking thing, I am unable to distinguish any parts within myself; I understand myself to be something quite single and complete . . . By contrast, there is no corporeal or extended thing that I can think of which in my thought I cannot easily divide into parts; and this very fact makes me understand that it is divisible. This one argument would be enough to show me that the mind is completely different from the body . . . (AT VII 85–6: CSM II 59)

This argument can be reformulated as follows, replacing 'mind' for 'I':

1. I understand the mind to be indivisible by its very nature.
2. I understand body to be divisible by its very nature.
3. Therefore, the mind is completely different from the body.

Notice the conclusion that mind and body are really distinct is not explicitly stated but can be inferred from 3. What is interesting about this formulation is how the Meditator reaches his conclusion. He does not assert a clear and distinct perception of these two natures as completely different but instead makes his point based on a particular property of each. However, this is not just any property but a property each has 'by its very nature'. Accordingly, the Meditator is claiming that divisibility is part of or contained in the nature or essence of extension, whereas indivisibility is part of or contained in the nature or essence of thinking.

The Meditator's line of reasoning for these claims about the respective natures of mind and body runs as follows. First, it is easy to see that bodies are divisible. Just take any body, say a pencil or a piece of paper, and then break it or cut it in half. Now there are two bodies instead of one. Second, based on this line of reasoning, it is easy to see why the Meditator believes that the mind is indivisible: if a mind or an 'I' could be divided, then two minds or 'I' would result; but since this 'I' just is myself, this would be the same as claiming that the division of the mind results in two selves, which is absurd. Therefore, the body is essentially divisible and the mind is essentially indivisible. But how does this lead to the conclusion that they are completely different?

Here it should be noted that a difference in just any non-essential property would have only shown that mind and body are not exactly the same. But this is a much weaker claim than the conclusion that they are completely different. For two things could have the same nature such as extension, for example, but have other, changeable properties or modes distinguishing them. Hence, these two rocks could be different in some respect (e.g. they may have different shapes), but this does not make them completely different, since both would still essentially be extended things. So, showing that mind and body are not exactly the same is not enough. He needs to take it further by establishing that mind and body have absolutely nothing in common and are, therefore, completely different. It is only from here that he can reach the further conclusion that mind and body do not require each other to exist but only the power of God.

This argument permits the Meditator to reach this stronger conclusion precisely because these essential attributes of mind and body, respectively, are contradictories. For if the nature of the mind, for example, were contained in the nature of the body, then the body's nature would have all of the same attributes as that contained in the nature of the mind. This would mean that one and the same nature, i.e. extension, would be both divisible and indivisible, which is unintelligible. Hence the fact that indivisibility is an essential attribute of the mind, and divisibility is an essential attribute of the body implies that they are not one and the same thing or even two things with the same nature, but that their natures are completely different. Taking this a step further, this implies that divisible body can be understood without indivisible mind and vice versa. Accordingly, each can be understood as existing all by itself: they are two really distinct substances.

However, unlike the Conceptual Argument, the Meditator does not invoke the doctrine of clear and distinct ideas to justify his premises. If he had, the Divisibility/Indivisibility Argument would also be absolutely certain from within his own epistemological framework. But if it is removed from this apparatus, it is possible that the Meditator is mistaken about the indivisibility of the mind, because the possibility of the mind requiring a brain to exist would still be a live option. Since under these circumstances extension would be part of the nature of the mind, it would then have to be divisible. As a result, the Meditator could not legitimately reach the conclusion that mind and body are completely different. This would also preclude the further conclusion that mind and body are really distinct substances. In the final analysis, the Meditator has not adequately eliminated the possibility of minds being bodily things like brains.[1]

7.3 THE MIND-BODY PROBLEM

The completely opposite natures of mind and body give rise to what many consider a very serious and even fatal flaw in Descartes' metaphysics. Gassendi expresses this problem in the following passage from the *Fifth Objections*:

> How can there be effort directed against anything, or motion set up in it, unless there is mutual contact between what moves and what is moved? And how can there be contact without a body when, as is transparently clear by the natural light, 'naught apart from body, can touch or yet be touched'? (AT VII 341: CSM II 237)

Here Gassendi's point is that the mind cannot cause the body to move, because its immaterial nature precludes it from coming into contact with the body, which is required for one thing to give motion to another. Interestingly enough, Princess Elizabeth of Bohemia raises the same concern in a letter dated 16 May 1645:

> I beseech you to tell me how the mind of man (being only a thinking substance) can determine the spirits of the body in order to make voluntary actions. For it seems that every determination of movement is made by the impulsion of the thing moved by the manner in which it is pushed by what moves it . . . (AT III 661; my translation)

Elizabeth goes on to say how contact is required for this to happen. For example, Jane might choose to go to the shop to buy groceries. This choosing is an act of will, which is then considered the cause of her moving her limbs (by standing up, getting her car keys, etc.) so as to buy groceries. But in the case of voluntary bodily movements, contact between mind and body would be impossible given the mind's non-extended nature. This is because contact must be between two surfaces, but surface is a mode of body. Accordingly, the mind does not have a surface that can come into contact with the body and cause it to move. So, it seems that if mind and body are completely different, there is no intelligible explanation of voluntary bodily movement.[2] This is commonly known as the problem of mind to body causal interaction.

Although Gassendi and Elizabeth limited themselves to the problem of voluntary bodily movement, a similar problem arises for sensations or the so-called problem of 'body to mind causation'. For instance, a visual sensation of a tree is commonly considered a mode of the mind alone. The cause of this mode would be explained by the motion of various imperceptible bodies causing parts of the eye to move, which would result in the sensory idea of the tree in the mind. But how can the movement of these minuscule bodily parts bring about the existence of a sensory idea when the mind is incapable of receiving modes of motion given its non-extended nature? Again, since the mind is incapable of having motion and a surface, no intelligible explanation of sensation seems possible either. Therefore, the completely different natures of mind and body seem to render their causal interaction impossible.

The main significance for Descartes' philosophy is that it undermines his claim to have a clear and distinct understanding of the mind without the body. For humans do have sensations and voluntarily move some of their bodily limbs and, if Gassendi and Elizabeth are correct, this requires a surface and contact. Since the mind must have a surface and a capacity for motion, the mind must also be extended and, therefore, mind and body are not completely different. This means the 'clear and distinct' ideas of mind and body, as mutually exclusive natures, must be false in order for mind-body causal interaction to occur. Hence, Descartes has not adequately established that mind and body are two really distinct substances.

However, despite the obviousness of this problem, and the amount of attention given to it, Descartes himself never took this issue very seriously. His response to Gassendi is a telling example:

> These questions presuppose amongst other things an explanation of the union between the soul and the body, which I have not yet dealt with at all. But I will say, for your benefit at least, that the whole problem contained in such questions arises simply from a supposition that is false and cannot in any way be proved, namely that, if the soul and the body are two substances whose nature is

different, this prevents them from being able to act on each other. (AT VII 213: CSM II 275)

It is noteworthy that here and in a letter to Elizabeth (see AT III 664–5: CSM K 218) Descartes maintains that an explanation of how mind and body are united is essential to addressing this issue. The doctrine of mind-body union will be addressed at length throughout the remaining three sections of this chapter. But first a brief account of the false supposition Descartes accuses Gassendi of maintaining is in order. In the latter part of the above passage, Descartes claims that Gassendi's supposition that 'two substances whose nature is different . . . prevents them from being able to act on each other' is false. Yet the issue, as expressed by both Gassendi and Elizabeth, does stem from a legitimate concern about how an immaterial mind can come into contact with the body. How is this supposition false?

This aspect of Descartes' response harks back to the causal principle deployed in the *Third Meditation* arguments for God's existence discussed in Chapters 3 and 4. Recall that what is more real cannot be caused by what is less real. On this account, a mode cannot cause a finite substance to exist and a finite substance cannot cause the existence of an infinite substance. But something can cause something on the same or a lower level of reality to exist such that finite substances can cause other finite substances as well as modes to exist. Now, voluntary bodily movements would be modes of the body and sensations would be modes of the mind. Therefore, a finite substance (i.e. the mind) would be causing modes of motion in the body; and modes of motion in the body would be causing the mental mode of sensation in the mind. Neither of these two scenarios violates the causal principle, because the effect is caused by something that is either as real (i.e. mode to mode) or more real (i.e. finite substance to mode) than it. Therefore, the completely diverse natures of mind and body do not violate the causal principle, which is supposed to apply only on the most general level of substances and modes. Accordingly, one of the suppositions upon which the problem of mind-body causal interaction rests is false.

One last thing should be acknowledged before moving on to Descartes' explanation of mind-body union. Notice that Gassendi and Elizabeth are attributing to Descartes a very particular theory about human nature, namely that a human being is not one substance but two completely separate and independent substances that causally interact by contact and motion. But an often overlooked text in the *Sixth Meditation* argues that this just isn't so, but rather, despite the possibility of the independent existence of mind and body, they are joined together not as two things that causally interact by contact and motion but as one, whole thing to form a human being. This often neglected passage is the subject of the next section.

7.4 THE SAILOR IN A SHIP ARGUMENT

Soon after the second argument for the real distinction between mind and body Descartes offers the following argument that mind and body are united to form one thing (*unum quid*):

> Nature also teaches me, by these sensations of pain, hunger, thirst and so on, that I am not merely present in my body as a sailor is present in a ship, but that I am very closely joined and, as it were, intermingled with it, so that I and the body form one thing (*unum quid*). If this were not so, I, who am nothing but a thinking thing, would not feel pain when the body was hurt, but would perceive the damage by the pure intellect (*pure intellectu*), just as a sailor perceives by sight if anything in his ship is broken. Similarly, when the body needed food or drink, I should have an explicit understanding of the fact, instead of having confused sensations of hunger and thirst. For these sensations of hunger, thirst, pain and so on are nothing but confused modes of thinking, which rise from the union, and, as it were, intermingling of the mind with the body. (AT VII 81: CSM II 56; translation modified)

The first sentence of this passage establishes the argument's conclusion that the mind (i.e. the 'I') and the body are not united as a sailor is present in his ship but rather in such a way as to form one thing. This, of course, raises a question about how these two completely different substances can become one thing. The sense in which this can happen given the limitations of the real distinction arguments will be addressed later in this section. But for now it is important to examine the line of reasoning used to reach this conclusion.

The next sentence states that if mind and body were not united to form one thing but were united as a sailor is present in his ship, then he would not have the confused modes of hunger, thirst and pain. He then expands on the analogy of a sailor in his ship. The point is that just as a sailor does not feel pain when his ship is damaged but sees it, so also if the mind were united to the body as a sailor is present in his ship, then the mind would not feel pain, for example, when the body was damaged. Instead it would perceive that something was wrong with the body by a pure intellectual perception of the motions in the body. Indeed, this is how an angel would perceive damage to a body if it were joined to a human body (see the letter to Descartes' wayward disciple, Regius, dated January 1642; AT III 493: CSM K 206). But since 'I' do have sensations of hunger, thirst and pain, this sort of union like a sailor is present in his ship is *not* the sort of union that obtains between me (i.e. the mind) and the body. Therefore, 'I' must be united to my body so as to form one thing.

Now that the argument itself has been summarized, several key features should be highlighted. First, the sailor in a ship analogy is not new with Descartes. It was commonly used to describe a conception of soul-body union that was commonly associated with Plato. Thomas Aquinas does just this in the following excerpt from his *Summa Contra Gentiles*:

> Accordingly, Plato and his followers asserted that the intellectual soul is not united to the body as form to matter, but only as mover to movable, for Plato said that the soul is in the body 'as a sailor in a ship'.[3]

Notice that here Aquinas characterizes the sailor in a ship view as asserting that the soul is united to the body in the same way as a mover is related to what is movable. This is precisely what Gassendi and Elizabeth assume in raising their objections about mind-body causal interaction – they assume that mind and body are two things actually existing apart and then one (i.e. the mind) moves the moveable limbs of the other. But Descartes explicitly rejects this sailor in a ship view of mind-body union in the argument just discussed, and therefore he rejects the mover-moveable relation as the relation constituting that union. The argument concludes that mind and body are united so as to form one thing, not two things that causally interact as mover and moveable.

This observation sheds light on why Descartes did not see Gassendi or Elizabeth's concerns about mind-body causal interaction as a serious problem. These two objectors are assuming a certain kind of causal relation (i.e. mover-moveable) between mind and body that Descartes had already rejected in the *Sixth Meditation*. Hence, Elizabeth and Gassendi's concern about contact and motion stems from a false assumption about the relation uniting mind and body to form a human being. Once this relation is made clear, the problem of mind-body causal interaction raised by Gassendi and Elizabeth disappears.

7.5 THE MODES OF MIND-BODY UNION

Although Descartes is rather short with Gassendi and the problems he raises about the causal interaction of mind and body, he is much more congenial with his royal correspondent, Princess Elizabeth of Bohemia. In his correspondence with Elizabeth, Descartes delicately tries to show her the false assumption upon which her concern is based by enumerating various 'primitive notions':

> First I consider that there are in us certain primitive notions which are as it were the patterns on the basis of which we form all our other conceptions. There are very few such notions . . . Then as regards body in particular, we have only the notion of extension, which entails the notions of shape and motion; and as regards the soul on its own, we have only the notion of thought, which includes the perceptions of the intellect and the inclinations of the will. Lastly, as regards the soul and the body together, we have only the notion of their union, on which depends our notion of the soul's power to move the body, and the body's power to act on the soul and cause its sensations and passions. (AT III 665: CSM K218)

First, notice that the primitive notions of body and mind each entail or include the notion of their respective kinds of modes. So, for instance, the notion of body entails shape and motion, while the notion of the soul includes only the notions of the modes of perception and will. Notice that the notion of body does not entail these notions of perceptions or volitions, nor does the notion of the soul entail these notions of bodily modes like motion. Hence these two primitive notions are mutually exclusive. Secondly, notice that the notion of mind-body union is also enumerated among this list of primitive notions with its own set of notions that depend on it, viz. those of voluntary bodily movement and sensations and passions. The parallel between the notion of mind-body union and those of body and soul taken individually suggests that the notions depending on it are also the modes arising from the soul-body composition just as the notions of size and motion, for example, are the notions of modes of extension.

This interpretation is supported by *Principles* I.48 where Descartes claims that hunger, thirst, emotions, passions and sensations should not be referred to the mind alone or to the body alone but arise 'from the close and intimate union of our mind with the body' (AT VIIIA 23: CSM I 209). It is also supported by the following passage from the *Sixth Meditation*:

> For this [i.e. the nature bestowed on me by God] includes many things that belong to the mind alone – for example my perception that what is done cannot be undone . . . but at this stage I am not speaking of these matters. It also includes much that relates to the body alone, like the tendency to move in a downward direction, and so on; but I am not speaking of these matters either. My sole concern here is with what God has bestowed on me as a combination of mind and body. (AT VII 82: CSM II 57)

In this passage as well, the Meditator distinguishes the various things that God has bestowed on his nature into three classes. The first are those things like intellectual perceptions that are bestowed on him insofar as he is a soul. The second class is composed of those things bestowed on him insofar as he is a body, e.g. motion. Finally, the third class is constituted by those things like pain that are bestowed on him as a *combination* of mind and body. This again suggests that pain and pleasure are modes of the mind-body composite. The textual evidence then supports the supposition that the notions that depend on the primitive notion of mind-body union in the letter to Elizabeth are the notions of its modes.

Moreover, given the considerations of the previous section, it implies that the union and therefore these modes do not arise because of a mover-moveable relation between mind and body, but rather they arise out of this one thing formed by their union. Some light can be shed on how this can occur from within Descartes' system by his discussion of the difference between invented natures and those that are true and immutable found in the *First Replies*. Recall from Chapter 4 that this discussion is in response to an objection to the ontological argument. However, this discussion also sheds light on the true and immutable natures of things and their deductive consequences. Here Descartes uses a triangle and a square as examples:

> But if I think of a triangle or a square . . . then whatever I apprehend as being contained in the idea of the triangle – for example

that its three angles are equal to two right angles – I can with truth assert of the triangle. And the same applies to the square with respect to whatever I apprehend as being contained in the idea of a square. (AT VII 117: CSM II 84)

Here Descartes is claiming that the concepts of true and immutable natures, like that of a triangle, have ideas contained in them that can be truthfully asserted about them. For example, the fact that a Euclidean triangle has angles equalling 180 degrees is contained in the idea of the triangle's nature. Since this is an immediate perception of a necessary connection between two ideas, the fact that its angles equal 180 degrees is a deduction made from the idea of the triangle's nature.

Descartes then goes on to apply this point to the idea of the nature of a triangle-inscribed-in-a-square:

Moreover, if I consider a triangle inscribed in a square, with a view not to attributing to the square properties that belong only to the triangle, or attributing to the triangle properties that belong to the square, but with a view to examining only the properties which arise out of the conjunction of the two, then the nature of this composite will be just as true and immutable as the nature of the triangle alone or the square alone. (AT VII 118: CSM II 84)

This passage has several interesting features germane to this discussion. First, composite natures like that of a triangle-inscribed-in-a-square also have demonstrable properties not possessed by either one of its parts alone. Second, the warning against ascribing the demonstrable properties of one part to the other indicates that the parts still have their respective properties, but a new set of demonstrable properties arises when these two parts are related in a certain way, viz. the relation of inscription. This suggests that the demonstrable properties of the whole nature of a triangle-inscribed-in-a-square are those of the triangle alone, those of the square alone, and those of the composite. Notice that this is reminiscent of what Descartes says about what God has bestowed on his nature in the *Sixth Meditation* quoted above where he distinguishes what belongs to the mind alone, the body alone and to the composite.

Several lessons can be drawn from the considerations of this and the previous section. First, the existence of certain modes, i.e. thirst, hunger and pain, implies the existence of a nature capable of having them. So just as the existence of modes of doubting and other thoughts implies the existence of a thinking nature that is capable of having them, so also the existence of modes of sensation and voluntary bodily movement implies the existence of a nature capable of having them, viz. the entity resulting from the union of mind and body. Second, just as with the nature of a triangle-inscribed-in-a-square, there must be a special relation that unites mind and body in such a way as to give rise to these capabilities. According to Descartes, this relation cannot be the mover-moveable relation characterized by the sailor in a ship analogy, but must be some other relation that gives rise to one, whole thing that is a true and immutable nature unto itself. Finally, all this points to the fact that the problem of mind-body causal interaction stems from mistakenly understanding the relation uniting mind and body as the relation of mover to moveable, which the Meditator had explicitly rejected in the *Sixth Meditation*.

7.6 ELIZABETH'S (AND GASSENDI'S) MISTAKE

As mentioned earlier, Descartes is rather impatient with Gassendi on this issue, but he is much more understanding of Princess Elizabeth. Indeed, Descartes goes to some pains to show Elizabeth how to understand the union of mind and body in such a way that her concern about their causal interaction will no longer trouble her. The doctrine of primitive notions just discussed is supposed to provide the basis for this new understanding. In this context, it is important to recognize that these primitive notions are just that – primitive:

> I observe that all human knowledge consists solely in clearly distinguishing these notions and attaching each of them only to the things to which it pertains. For if we try to solve a problem by means of a notion that does not pertain to it, we cannot help going wrong. Similarly we go wrong if we try to explain one of these notions by another, for since they are primitive notions, each of them can be understood only through itself. (AT III 665–6: CSM K 218)

The last sentence shows why these notions are primitive, namely that each must be understood through itself and cannot be understood through any other primitive notion. As such, primitive notions form the basis or patterns of other knowledge. This means, then, that the notion of mind-body union cannot be entirely understood through the primitive notion of the soul, that of the body or the mere conjunction of the two but only through itself just as any other primitive notion. Another important feature of this passage is Descartes' exhortation to keep these notions separate from one another and how problems can be solved only through the notion pertaining to the issue at hand. Descartes gives the following examples to make his point:

> For instance, we try to use our imagination to conceive the nature of the soul, or we try to conceive the way in which the soul moves the body by conceiving the way in which one body is moved by another. (AT III 666: CSM K218)

Any attempt to imagine the soul is an attempt to picture it in the mind using spatial dimensions, but this would be to make the mistake of trying to understand the soul through the notion of the body.

In the second example, Descartes claims that any attempt to understand how the mind moves the body (i.e. voluntary bodily movement) through the notion of body is a mistake. Notice that this is precisely what gave rise to the problem for both Elizabeth and Gassendi. They both were puzzled about how an immaterial mind or soul, which cannot have a surface, could come into contact with the body to make it move. This indicates that understanding voluntary bodily movement in this way is a mistake, for it is to conceive how the mind moves the body in the same way as one body moves another. So the source of the mind-body causal interaction problem, as it was understood by Elizabeth and Gassendi, is their mistaken understanding of the mind-body relation as that of the mover-moveable relation, which is the same relation one body has to another. As a result, the problem of mind-body causal interaction disappears once this assumption is rejected. For once the supposition that the mind must move the body as one body moves another is removed, the concerns about a surface and contact are no longer pertinent.

7.7 THE MIND-BODY RELATION

This chapter has examined two theses about Descartes' understanding of how mind and body are related. The first is that mind and body are two really distinct substances, while the second is that they are united so as to form one whole thing that is a true and immutable nature in its own right, viz. a human being. This gives rise to another problem: how can a human being be both two things (i.e. a mind and a body) and one thing? Descartes addresses this concern in another letter to Princess Elizabeth dated 28 June 1643:

> It does not seem to me that the human mind is capable of forming a very distinct conception of both the distinction between the soul and the body and their union; for to do this it is necessary to conceive them as a single thing and at the same time to conceive them as two things; and this is absurd. (AT III 693: CSMK227)

Why would Descartes maintain a thesis that he considers absurd? The answer to this question is found in the fact that the problem arises when a human being is conceived both in terms of the whole and in terms of the parts at one and the same time. But the whole can be considered at one time without reference to the parts as the parts can be considered individually without reference to the whole. For instance, in the case of a triangle-inscribed-in-a-square, the whole nature and its demonstrable properties can be considered at one time, while the triangle and its demonstrable properties can be understood all by itself at another, and similarly for the square. Likewise, the whole human being (i.e. mind-body composite) and its demonstrable properties (i.e. capacities for modes of voluntary bodily movement, sensation and the passions) can be considered at one time, while the parts constituting this whole can be considered individually at another time.

This, however, still does not address the apparently absurd conclusion that a human being is both two distinct things and one, whole thing. This issue can be resolved by remembering exactly what the real distinction and the Sailor in a Ship Arguments were supposed to show. The former concludes only that the mind *can* exist independently of the body and vice versa, while the latter argues that they *are* united in such a way as to give rise to one, whole thing with its own set of demonstrable properties. Descartes says just this in the following excerpt from the *Fourth Replies*:

> I do not think I proved too much in showing that the mind *can* exist apart from the body. Nor do I think I proved too little in saying that the mind *is* substantially united with the body, since that substantial union does not prevent our having a clear and

distinct concept of the mind on its own, as a complete thing. (AT VII 228: CSM II 160; emphasis added)

The fact that mind and body are substantially united to form one, whole thing does not mean that the mind is not really distinct from the body, because even though mind and body actually are united in this way, it is still possible for them to exist separately at least by the power of God.

This passage also sheds some light on a glaring omission the reader may have noticed, namely that although the fact that mind and body are not united as mover to moveable has been shown, no positive account of the union has been provided thus far. In the passage just cited Descartes is referring to the Sailor in a Ship Argument discussed at 7.4 and claims to have proven that the mind is 'substantially united' with the body. Although this is not the place for a thorough examination of this concept as found in Descartes' philosophy, suffice it to say that 'substantial union' was a common, scholastic term denoting the union between a substantial form and matter. On this account, mind and body do not bear a primarily efficient causal relation, as would be the case if they were united as mover to moveable, but rather the mind bears a formal causal relation to the body. But this is to exchange one problem for another: how can an immaterial soul act on a body for the sake of actualizing its potential for being human? This is a problem for just about every form-matter theory of soul-body union. But an answer to this question has yet to be found.[4]

7.8 HUMAN LIFE

Descartes makes several other interesting and important remarks about this human being that is composed of a united mind and body. This section sketches three of these further points. First, despite his aversion to final causes, Descartes is explicit that humans have certain perceptions, viz. sensations and passions, because of the goal of self-preservation. Second, the cryptic dictum about the soul being wholly in the whole body and the whole in each of its parts briefly mentioned at 3.8 will be examined and some sense of it will be made. Finally, the manner in which human death occurs will also be briefly discussed. The discussions of these three issues will serve both to round out Descartes' theory of human nature as well as to provide a good starting point for understanding his theories of sensation, the passions and morals discussed in Chapter 8.

First, remember that Descartes rejects final causal explanations in physics. One major reason for this was that the use of final causes was the result of an illicit ascription of mental properties to entirely non-mental things like stones. This implies that it would be legitimate to ascribe final causes to things endowed with mentality. Now, although a human being is not entirely a mind, it is still essentially a mental thing, since the mind or soul is part of its true and immutable nature. The Meditator does just this when he mentions the purpose of sensations in the *Sixth Meditation*:

> For the proper purpose of the sensory perceptions given me by nature is simply to inform the mind of what is beneficial or harmful for the composite of which the mind is a part; and to this extent they are sufficiently clear and distinct. (AT VII 83: CSM II 57)

So the goal of preserving the mind-body composite, i.e. sustaining one's own life as a human being, explains why humans are organized in such a way as to have sensory perceptions. This is also the purpose or proper function of passions such as love, hatred, desire, joy and sadness:

> Regarding this, it must be observed that they are all ordained by nature to relate to the body, and to belong to the soul only in so far as it is joined with the body. Hence, their natural function is to move the soul to consent and contribute to the actions which may serve to preserve the body or render it in some way more perfect. (AT XI 429–30: CSM I 376)

This excerpt from *Passions of the Soul* II.137 indicates that the passions are explained by their goal of promoting the preservation and perfection of the human body (in the strict sense of 'human body' discussed at 3.8). The final causal aspect of the human composite is important for several reasons. First, it provides some (though not conclusive) evidence in support of the form-matter account of Descartes' theory of mind-body union discussed above because of the central role of final causes in all such composites. Second, these passages indicate that sensation and passions arise from the mind-body union for the sake of preserving that union. Hence, sensation and passion, which are, strictly speaking, modes of the mind-body composite, are best understood as providing some of the means for attaining this end.

The second issue is the cryptic doctrine of 'the whole in the whole and the whole in any one of its parts'. This statement is found in the *Sixth Replies* where Descartes compares the sense in which the soul is 'coextensive' with the body with the way in which the scholastics maintained that the 'real accident' of gravity or heaviness was coextensive with a body like a stone:

> I saw that the gravity, while remaining coextensive with the heavy body, could exercise all its force in any one part of the body, for if the body were hung from a rope attached to any part of it, it would still pull the rope down with all its force, just as if all the gravity existed in the part actually touching the rope instead of scattered throughout the remaining parts. This is exactly the way in which I now understand the mind to be coextensive with the body – the whole mind in the whole body and the whole mind in any one of its parts. (AT VII 442: CSM II 298)

Unfortunately, this is not the place for a detailed analysis of this passage. But for present purposes, an important feature of it is that even though gravity was thought by the Scholastics to be coextensive with the stone in that it is found wholly in the whole stone and wholly in any one of its parts, it could still exercise all its power from just one point. Hence, a stone hung at one point from a rope still pulls downward with all the same force as it would were the entire stone involved.

What this means for the mind-body composite is best understood through the resolution of another aspect of Descartes' theory that occurs most explicitly at *Passions* I.30 and 31. In section 30, Descartes states that 'the soul is united to all of the parts of the body conjointly', which is just a simpler way of stating that the whole soul is in the whole body. But sections 31 and 32, though admitting that the whole soul is in the whole body, claim that the soul performs its functions more particularly in the pineal gland, located at the centre of the brain, where it has its principal seat (AT XI 351–3: CSM I 339–40). This raises the following question among scholars: how can the soul be united to the whole body yet only be in the pineal gland?

The answer to this question is found in two previous points made in Chapter 2 about the mind and its functions. First, the mind is the human soul for Descartes, and as such it is the principle of rational, human life. In this context, the mind animates a human body so as to make it a living human body. In this way, the whole mind must be in the whole body in order for the entire body to be truly alive. Here it is important to notice that the whole body is alive and not just one part of it. Hence, the soul is, to this extent, wholly in the whole body and wholly in any one of its parts in that both the parts and the whole of a human body are alive. Indeed, to maintain that the soul is wholly in just one part of the body, e.g. the heart as many had maintained, would be to say that only the heart is alive while the rest of the body is not, which is absurd.

However, it is also difficult to overestimate the importance of the pineal gland in Descartes' physiology (see 8.1). But this can be reconciled by remembering that Descartes is not claiming that the mind is entirely in the pineal gland to the exclusion of any other body part but only that this is where the mind performs its proper functions most particularly. The fact that perception and will are the main functions of the mind is the other point from Chapter 2 that can help here. Descartes' physiology makes it clear that sensory perceptions and passions are received from the body through the pineal gland as are the actions of the will or volitions transmitted to the body through it. Therefore, the whole soul is in the whole body and the whole in any one of its parts by virtue of its function as a soul or animating principle, but it has its principal seat in the pineal gland insofar as the mind exercises its primary powers of perception and volition through it.

The third and final issue to be discussed is Descartes' account of death. Recall from the discussion of the soul's immortality at 4.6 and the Eucharist at 4.7 that for Descartes:

> [T]he human body, in so far as it differs from other bodies, is simply made up of a certain configuration of limbs and other accidents of this sort . . . (AT VII 14: CSM II 10)

A human body has a certain configuration of extended parts that makes it a human body, whereas another configuration of extended parts would result in some other kind of body, e.g. the body of a dog, cat, tree or housefly. Recall further that, strictly speaking, a human body is one that is substantially united to a soul, which implies that a truly human body is alive. Descartes then distinguishes a living human body from a dead one at *Passions* I.6:

> So as to avoid error, let us note that death never occurs through

the absence of the soul, but only because one of the principal parts of the body decays. (AT XI 330: CSM I 329)

He goes on to compare a living human body to a watch that is working correctly and a dead human body to a watch that is broken (see AT XI 331: CSM I 329). It would be easy to interpret this comparison to mean that the human body is nothing but a mechanism without a soul like a watch. But such an understanding would be the result of not reading the passage closely enough. Descartes' point has less to do with the watch's status as a machine than with the fact that a dead body is like a broken watch. When a watch is broken, it is no longer able to keep time. Similarly, when some principal part of the human body decays, it is in some sense 'broken'. Since the body is now broken it can no longer sustain a union with the soul. Hence, the soul's leaving does not kill the body, but rather the body's broken parts make it impossible for it to sustain its union with the soul. On this account, the body is corrupted, while the soul can continue to live on without it. This then allows Descartes to focus on the human body (in the strict sense) and its preservation when developing his physiology.

CHAPTER 8

SENSATIONS, PASSIONS AND MORALITY

This chapter takes a look at some of the branches that spring from the trunk of physics found on Descartes' philosophical tree. Although the branches of mechanics and medicine are not explicitly addressed here, these principles manifest themselves in the first two sections concerning the physiology of sensation and the passions. The next two sections look at Descartes' earlier and later moral theories, which are based squarely on his physiological theories and how the will can exercise its powers over the passions. The final section provides some concluding remarks.

8.1 THE PHYSIOLOGY OF SENSATION

Recall from 2.5 and 7.8 that Descartes argues that minds or souls are, strictly speaking, immaterial principles of rational, human life. But those faculties by which animals are considered alive, viz. nutrition and sensation, are not 'souls' strictly speaking, since they can be explained by the configuration and motion of non-thinking, material parts. Descartes claims in his *World* that these faculties can be explained in the same way in humans:

> the [human] body [is] nothing but a statue or machine made of earth, which God forms with the explicit intention of making it as much as possible like us. Thus God not only gives it externally the colours and shapes of all the parts of our bodies, but also places inside it all the parts required to make it walk, eat, breathe, and indeed to imitate all those of our functions which can be imagined to proceed from matter and so depend solely on the disposition of our organs. (AT XI 120: CSM I 99)

The same point is made again in his later, unpublished work entitled *Description of the Human Body*. Here Descartes argues that different faculties of the human soul should not be postulated in order to explain bodily functions that do not require an act of will or volition:

> [W]hen all the bodily organs are appropriately disposed for some movement, the body has no need of the soul in order to produce that movement; and, as a result, all movements which we in no way experience as depending on our thought must be attributed not to the soul, but simply to the disposition of the organs. (AT XI 225: CSM I 315)

Here and earlier in this work Descartes acknowledges that some functions require a mind, e.g. voluntary bodily movement, while others do not. So, for Descartes, the human body, to the extent that its functions do not require thinking, is a machine just like the bodies of animals.

In his last published work, *The Passions of the Soul*, Descartes provides accounts of how various motions in the body give rise to certain sensations and passions or emotions. Recall from 7.8 that for Descartes the mind or soul performs its principle functions in the pineal gland located near the centre of the brain. Descartes justifies his choice of the pineal gland or *conarium* in a letter of 21 April 1641 to Mersenne:

> It is certain too that the seat of the common sense must be very mobile, to receive all the impressions which come from the senses; but it must also be of such a kind as to be movable only by the spirits which transmit these impressions. Only the *conarium* [i.e. pineal gland] fits this description. (AT III 362: CSMK 180)

Hence, Descartes places the common sense, which was traditionally thought to be where the data from the five senses became united into a single experience, in the pineal gland.[1] This is because he believes that only the pineal gland is mobile enough to receive all and only the movements of the so-called 'animal spirits'.

This doctrine of the animal spirits, though a little strange to us, is not new with Descartes. In fact, he seems to accept the traditional theory that associates animal spirits with the nervous system. For Descartes, nerves are very fine fibres encased in little pipes that extend and branch out from the brain to the extremities of the body. These fibres float in a very fine matter known as the 'animal spirits', which Descartes believed the brain makes out of blood. These animal spirits allow the nerve fibres to float freely so that anything causing the slightest motion anywhere in the body will cause movement in that part of the brain where the fibre is attached.[2] This movement then gives rise to a certain sensation in the mind.

The Meditator helps illustrate this physiology of sensation in the *Sixth Meditation*. Here he remarks that a cord marked ABCD can be pulled at the D end so as to make the A end move. But the movement of the A end of the cord can also be brought about by a similar movement at B or C. He then applies this general model to pain in the foot:

> When the nerves are pulled in the foot, they in turn pull on inner parts of the brain to which they are attached, and produce a certain motion in them; and nature has laid it down that this motion should produce in the mind a sensation of pain, as occurring in the foot. (AT VII 87: CSM II 60)

So a sensation of pain occurs *as if* it was in the foot, but it does not really occur there. Rather, only certain motions occur in the foot that are transmitted via the fibres or cords that are the nerves to the brain. The appropriate parts of the brain, and ultimately the pineal gland, are then set in motion in such a way that the sensation of 'pain in the foot' is produced. Descartes also uses his theory to explain the perplexing phenomenon of phantom limbs:

> [E]ven if it is not the part in the foot but one of the intermediate parts which is being pulled, the same motion will occur in the brain as occurs when the foot is hurt, and so it will necessarily come about that the mind feels the same sensation of pain. (AT VII 87: CSM II 60)

According to this passage, someone can feel pain as though it were in the foot even though the foot itself was never moved in the appropriate way or even exists. For example, someone who lost a foot in an accident will often report that his foot hurts. But how can his foot hurt if there's no foot and therefore no nerves to be moved? Descartes' explanation is that the same motion is occurring at some intermediate point along the nerve that once (but no longer) ran from the foot to the brain. This theory of the nervous system is Descartes' fundamental model for all sensation.

8.2 THREE GRADES OF SENSORY RESPONSE

This physiological picture of Descartes' theory of sensation can be expanded through his discussion of the three grades of sensory response in the *Sixth Replies*. These grades are as follows:

Grade 1: Immediate stimulation of bodily organs.
Grade 2: Sensations themselves such as the perception of pain, thirst, colour, etc.
Grade 3: Judgements made about those sensations.

Grade 1 only concerns the physiological process whereby sensations arise. Descartes uses the example of a stick immersed in water. The first grade occurs when light is reflected off the stick into the eye, which causes the animal spirits in the optic nerve to move. This motion then causes the pineal gland to move in a certain way, which gives rise to the sensation of seeing a stick immersed in water. This sensation itself constitutes the second grade of sensation, which can only arise in a mind united with a body (AT VII 437: CSM II 294). Most scholars take this to mean that sensations are modes of the mind alone insofar as it is in a mechanistic causal relation with the body. However, it is better to understand this to mean that sensations are not modes of the mind alone but are modes of the whole, mind-body composite since the capacity for sensation is a deductive consequence of this true and immutable nature as discussed at 7.5.[3]

Grade 3 concerns judgements made about the sensation that arose at Grade 2. Descartes continues with his example of the stick in water to make his point:

> But suppose that, as a result of being affected by this sensation of colour, I judge that a stick, located outside me, is coloured; and suppose that on the basis of the extension of the colour and its boundaries together with its position in relation to the parts of the brain, I make a rational calculation about the size, shape and distance of the stick . . . (AT VII 437: CSM II 295)

This passage harks back to the wax example discussed at 2.6 where Descartes argued that judgement is an integral part of sensation. It was discovered that the belief that the wax after being moved close to the fire was the same as before it was moved is not based on sensation or imagination but on judgement. Also recall from Chapter 5 that judgement is a faculty of the mind alone, resulting from the interplay of intellect and will. So, based on the understanding of what is presented in the sensation, the will chooses to affirm certain calculations about the stick's size, shape and distance. These judgements, then, are modes of the mind alone. Therefore, the physiological process at Grade 1 is comprised of entirely extended modes of size, shape and motion, while the sensations occurring at Grade 2 are modes of the whole composite, and finally the judgements occurring at Grade 3 are entirely mental in nature.

Descartes goes on to argue that this is how errors in sensation are corrected. For example, the refraction of the light off the stick immersed in water may cause the sensation of seeing the stick as bent. This sensory idea would then be materially false for Descartes, because it provides material for error; that is, it could entice someone without mature reasoning skills to judge that the stick is bent when it is not. But a mature mind can correct this error by judging that the stick is straight based on other evidence and previous experience, e.g. having previously discovered that straight sticks appear bent in the water (AT VII 438–9: CSM II 295–6). Thus sensations do not provide clear and distinct perceptions of the material world but only ones that are confused and could lead the incautious into error. However, despite this shortcoming, they still serve an important purpose. Again, recall from 7.8 that humans have sensations for the sake of providing the material for making judgements about what is good or bad for the survival or perfection of the composite human being.[4]

8.3 PASSIONS

The passions also have a role to play in the preservation and perfection of the human composite. In *Passions of the Soul*, Descartes lays out a moral theory based on his physiological theories of sensation and emotion. This section takes a brief look at Descartes' doctrine of the passions in general, while the final two sections of this chapter take short looks at his moral theory. Descartes begins this work by explaining what he means by the term 'passion' itself:

> In the first place, I note that whatever takes place or occurs is generally called by philosophers a 'passion' with regard to the subject to which it happens and an 'action' with regard to that which makes it happen. Thus, although an agent and patient are often

quite different, an action and passion must always be a single thing which has these two names on account of the two different subjects to which it may be related. (AT XI 328: CSM I 328)

Here Descartes takes a fairly standard scholastic-Aristotelian position on the nature of action and passion in general. Something that happens is called an 'action' when taken from the perspective of the agent that makes it happen, while that same happening is called a 'passion' when taken from the perspective of the patient or the recipient of the action. So, the terms 'action' and 'passion' are just two different ways of describing one and the same occurrence. For instance, the act of drawing a horse on a piece of paper is the same as the passion of the paper having a horse drawn on it. Notice that the same occurrence is being described first from the perspective of the person drawing and then from the perspective of the paper that is being drawn upon. So, according to Descartes, any passion of the soul is also an action of the body (see *Passions* I.2; AT XI 328: CSM I 328).

Later Descartes reiterates the two genera of thought discussed at 2.3. He denotes volition or will as the active faculty of the soul and perception as its passive faculty (see AT XI 342–343: CSM I 335–6). The passions of the soul are then defined at *Passions* I.27:

[I]t seems to me that we may define [the passions of the soul] generally as those perceptions, sensations or emotions of the soul which we refer particularly to it, and which are caused, maintained and strengthened by some movement of the spirits. (AT XI 349: CSM I 338–9)

The claim that passions are perceptions follows quite readily from the fact that this is the mind's passive faculty. But it is also important to distinguish passions from other sorts of perception such as evident knowledge. Descartes indicates that knowledge has very little to do with the passions in themselves, and that those who are most passionate are usually those who do not know their passions very well. Passions can also be called 'sensations' to the extent that they occur physiologically in the same way as sensations. But they are more properly called emotions (AT XI 349–50: CSM I 339).

Descartes goes on to explain this definition a little further:

I add that they refer particularly to the soul, in order to distinguish them from other sensations, some referred to external objects (e.g. smells, sounds and colours) and others to our body (e.g. hunger, thirst and pain). (AT XI 350: (SMI 339))

In this excerpt from *Passions* I.29, a difficulty arises concerning the nature of this reference, for notice that some sensations, like smell and sound, are referred to external objects, like flowers and bells, while sensations like hunger, thirst and pain are referred to the body, e.g. hunger occurs in the stomach or a pain occurs in the foot. Exactly what Descartes means by the 'reference' of these various sensations is difficult to discern. But presumably he means that the qualities represented in these sensory ideas are taken to be found in their respective referents. For instance, people often believe that the smell of a flower or the sourness of a lemon is found in the flower or the lemon itself. The same is true with the sensation of pain. When people feel a pain in their foot, they believe that the pain is actually in the foot. But, interestingly enough, Descartes considers both of these references to be mistakes. For recall that sensible qualities like smell and taste are mere ideas in the mind and are not found in things themselves. Moreover, as discussed at 8.1, the sensation of pain in the foot does not really occur in the foot but in the brain. This implies that passions such as joy or sadness are believed to be in the soul just as sourness was believed to be in the lemon or pain was believed to be in the foot. Yet, as with sourness and pain, this reference of these passions to the soul would also be mistaken.

Unfortunately, this very interesting implication cannot be explored any further here due to space restriction. However, if this reference of the passions to the soul is, strictly speaking, a mistake, then the question would arise as to where the passion really takes place. An interesting speculation is that, like Grade 2 sensations, the passions might also properly occur in the pineal gland, which would mean that they would be modes of the whole human being as well. The fact that passions are like sensations, in that both occur by the same physiological process, makes this a hypothesis worthy of further consideration. But the argumentation to establish this conclusion is too far beyond the scope of the present work to be attempted here. However, for now an example of the particular passions of anxiety, fear and courage should prove helpful.

After describing how the image of an animal comes through the two eyes to be united into one image in the pineal gland, Descartes gives a nice example of how the passions of anxiety, fear or courage may arise:

If, in addition, this shape [i.e. the image of the animal] is very strange and terrifying – that is, if it has a close relation to things which have previously been harmful to the body – this arouses the passion of anxiety in the soul, and then that of courage or perhaps fear and terror, depending upon the particular temperament of the body or the strength of the soul, and upon whether we have protected ourselves previously by defence or by flight against the harmful things to which the present impression is related. (AT XI 356: CSM I 342)

Notice that this passage presupposes that the first two grades of sensory response have already been achieved. The soul then makes a judgement based, perhaps, on prior experience that the animal depicted in the sensory idea is harmful to the body. In this way, the sensation is satisfying its goal or purpose of providing material to the mind for making judgements about the well-being of the human body (in the strict sense discussed at 4.6). This is reiterated in the following excerpt from *Passions* II.2:

The function of all the passions consists solely in this, that they dispose our soul to want the things which nature deems useful for us, and to persist in this volition . . . (AT XI 372: CSM I 349)

Returning to the example, the judgement that the animal might be harmful gives rise to anxiety and then to either courage or fear depending on the 'temperament of the body' or the 'strength of the soul'. Hence, whether courage or fear arises depends on the human being having that sensation and the feeling of anxiety.

Descartes elaborates on how this might happen:

Thus in certain persons these factors dispose their brain in such a way that some of the [animal] spirits reflected from the image formed on the [pineal] gland proceed from there to the nerves which serve to turn the back and move the legs in order to flee. The rest of the spirits go to nerves which expand or constrict the orifices of the heart, or else to nerves which agitate other parts of the body from which blood is sent to the heart, so that the blood is rarefied in a different manner from usual and spirits are sent to the brain which are adapted for maintaining and strengthening the passion of fear. (AT XI 356–7: CSM I 342)

This passage describes how the passions of anxiety and fear would affect someone with a certain disposition such that the animal spirits are moved from the pineal gland to the nerves that would cause the muscles to move in such a way that the person turns his back and runs away. Other animal spirits then affect the heart in such a way as to make the fear stronger as he runs away. Notice the reciprocal nature of the passions: they are first caused by the process of sensation, including its physiological aspect at Grade 1, and then those passions can turn around and have a physiological effect that results in certain bodily movements, like running, for 'the same agitation of the spirits which normally causes the passions also disposes the body to make movements which help us to attain these things' (AT XI 372: CSM I 349). Another interesting feature of this example is that whether the passion of anxiety results in the passion of fear or courage depends on the physical and/or mental disposition of the human being involved. This explains not only why different people under the same circumstances may feel differently but also why they would act differently as well (see AT XI 358–9: CSM I 343).

It is, however, also important to recognize that not only do the animal spirits move the pineal gland, but the mind, through an act of volition, also moves it in such a way that the animal spirits are driven to the muscles so as to move the legs or arms as willed (AT XI 3 60–1: CSM I 343–4). The mind can also have some power over the passions but only indirectly. Descartes again uses the example of fear:

[I]n order to arouse boldness and suppress fear in ourselves, it is not sufficient to have the volition to do so. We must apply ourselves to consider the reasons, objects, or precedents which persuade us that the danger is not great; that there is always more security in defence than flight . . . (AT XI 363: CSM I 345)

Here Descartes observes that the mere volition or desire to be bold or courageous is not enough for the passion itself to arise. Instead, the mind must actively consider other ideas, which, in turn, will allow fear to be overcome and replaced by courage. But the mind does not have full control over the passions because of the physiological process that strengthens them. When this happens, Descartes believes that the best people can do is to resist the action that normally accompanies a given passion: 'For example, if anger causes the hand to rise to strike a blow, the will can usually restrain it; if fear moves the legs in flight, the will can stop them; and similarly in other cases' (AT XI 364: CSM I 345).

Descartes also maintains that each volition is joined to some movement of the pineal gland such that the will to walk in one direction will cause the pineal gland to move in a certain way, which, in turn, causes the animal spirits to move to the muscles in such a way as to bring about the effect of walking in that direction. However, through effort and habit, that same volition may be joined to different movements. Hence, through repeated practice a natural connection between a volition and a movement of the pineal gland can be changed so that the same volition results in a different movement. This is reminiscent of the mental exercises Descartes recommends for remembering long deductions discussed at 1.5. Just as the mind could come to better remember long deductions, so also the mind can come to have better or even absolute control of the passions through repeated practice (AT XI 368–9: CSM I 348). For example, a person naturally disposed to flee when the passions of anxiety and fear arise can train herself to feel courage when that same anxiety arises so as to change the disposition for action from flight to fight.

Descartes believes that this practised rational control over the passions makes people better and more moral. This is achieved once the person has reached a state Descartes calls '*générosité*', which is the centrepiece of his mature moral philosophy. But a short look at the earlier, provisional moral code laid out in the earlier *Discourse* will show that Descartes' commitment to rational control and free choice runs deep with roots in his earlier thought.

8.4 THE PROVISIONAL MORAL CODE

In Part IV of the *Discourse*, Descartes lays out a provisional moral code to live by while engaged in his methodological doubt. He establishes this code of 'three or four' rules or maxims so that he is not frozen by uncertainty in the non-philosophical, practical affairs of life. These maxims can be paraphrased as follows:

1. To obey the laws and customs of my country, holding constantly to the Catholic religion, and governing myself in all other matters according to the most moderate opinions accepted in practice by the most sensible people.
2. To be as firm and decisive in action as possible and to follow even the most doubtful opinions once they have been adopted.

3. Try to master myself rather than fortune, and change my desires rather than the order of the world.
4. Review the various professions and choose the best. (AT VI 23–8: CSM I 122–5)

Before explaining each maxim, it is important to notice that this moral code is 'provisional'. Its provisional nature may stem from several of its features. First, it seems to be a temporary code to be followed when engaged in the project of methodological doubt. Presumably, once these doubts are overcome and an absolutely certain foundation for knowledge is discovered, another, absolutely certain moral code will take its place. Second, it may be considered 'provisional' in that these rules will probably (though not certainly) direct someone towards leading a happy and moral life. Bearing the probable nature of this code in mind, a look at each maxim is now in order.

The main thrust of the first maxim is to live a moderate and sensible life despite the uncertainty of his previously held beliefs. The rest of the maxim is intended to provide guidelines for achieving this moderate life. The first guideline is to live in accordance with the laws and customs of the country in which he resides because of the improbability of them leading him astray into an unhappy and sinful life. The second guideline is to follow the actions of sensible people, who avoid the extremes and take the middle road, for again, moderate actions are less likely to be wrong than extreme ones. Descartes is also sure to highlight that this guideline concerns moderate and sensible actions and not mere words, for people often say one thing and do another. Accordingly, a moderate and sensible person is not someone who preaches these virtues but someone who acts on and lives by them.

The third guideline found in the first maxim is to stick with his religious beliefs. This may seem inconsistent since religious beliefs would seem to fall within the scope of methodological doubt. But, interestingly enough, Descartes does not bring his religious beliefs into doubt in the *Discourse*. This is indicated by the fact that he does not employ the evil god scenario in this early work but only in the later *Meditations*. This scenario for doubt can be taken as bringing the existence of God into doubt in that the Meditator supposes for the sake of argument that God did not create him but maybe he was created by a being with all the perfections of God except that he is a deceiver. But the extent to which this can be seen as doubting religious beliefs is unclear. For now, suffice to say that since religious beliefs can be accepted on faith without absolutely certain rational justification, they are not subject to methodological doubt as employed in the *Discourse*. Accordingly, his religious beliefs can also serve as guides for moral conduct during this period of doubt.

The second maxim expresses a firmness of action so as to avoid the inaction produced by hesitation and uncertainty. Descartes uses the example of a traveller lost in a forest. This traveller should not wander about or even stand still for then he will never find his way. Instead, he should keep walking in a straight line and should never change his direction for slight reasons. Even though the traveller may not end up where he wants to be, at least he will be better off than in the middle of a forest. Similarly, since practical action must usually be performed without delay, there usually is not time to discover the truest or most certain course of action, but one must follow the most probable route. Even if no route seems most probable, some route must be chosen and resolutely acted upon and treated as the most true and certain in order to make any progress at all. But whatever route is chosen, it should not be changed for slight reasons. Such frequent changes of mind would result in a series of false starts but no determinate action. So it is best to choose the route understood at the outset to be the most likely to lead to success without second thoughts and with the confidence that the decision was the best to be made at the time. By following this maxim, Descartes hopes to avoid the regrets experienced by those who set out on a supposedly good course that they later judge to be bad.

In the third maxim Descartes proposes to master himself rather than fortune. This is based on the realization that all that is in his control are his own thoughts and nothing else, which means that just about everything else is out of his control. This has several implications. First, if he has done his best but fails to achieve something, then it follows that it was not within his power to achieve it. This is because his own best efforts were not sufficient to achieve that end, and so whatever effort would be sufficient to achieve it is beyond his abilities. The second implication is that he should desire only those things that are within his power to obtain, and so he should control his desires rather than try to master things beyond his control. Therefore, if some end cannot be achieved with his best efforts, he should choose not to desire that end any more and direct his efforts elsewhere. In this way, Descartes hopes to avoid the regret experienced by those who have desires that they cannot satisfy such that one should not desire health when ill nor freedom when imprisoned. Notice that in this maxim Descartes is not only acknowledging that many things are beyond his control, but he is also promoting rational control over oneself. This is central to his doctrine of the passions discussed above and the notion of *générosité* to be discussed in 8.5 below.

It is difficult to see why the fourth maxim is included. Indeed, Descartes himself seems hesitant about including it when he states at the outset that his provisional moral code consists of 'three or four maxims'. But surely the choice of an occupation is important for anyone who has to work for a living. However, Descartes claims never to have seriously considered other occupations and that he is content with his current work because of the pleasure he receives from discovering new and not widely known truths. This implies that the correct choice of occupation can ensure a degree of contentedness that could not be otherwise achieved if one is engaged in an occupation for which one is not suited. Descartes also claims that his current occupation is the basis of the other three maxims, because it is his current plan to continue his instruction that gave rise to them. He concludes with a brief discussion of how his occupational path leads to the acquisition of knowledge, which, in turn, will lead to all the true goods within his grasp. His final point is that learning how best to judge what is good and bad makes it possible to act well and achieve all attainable virtues and goods. Happiness is assured when this point is reached with certainty. In the *Passions* of 1649, this manifests itself as the virtue of *générosité*.

8.5 *GÉNÉROSITÉ*

After the *Discourse* of 1637, Descartes did not take up the issue of morality in any significant way again until his correspondence with Princess Elizabeth in 1643, which culminated in his remarks about *générosité* in the *Passions of the Soul*. Given the temporal distance between his main reflections on morality, it is easy to attribute to Descartes two moral systems – the provisional moral code and the ethics of *générosité*. But Descartes' later moral thinking retains versions of the second and third maxim although without much mention of the first and fourth. This indicates that Descartes' later moral theory is really an extension of his earlier thought with the second and third maxims at its core.

Générosité is discussed in some detail at *Passions* III.153. Here Descartes claims that *générosité* 'causes a person's self-esteem to be as great as it may legitimately be', and that it has two components.

The first is knowing that only the freedom to dispose volitions is in anyone's power. Accordingly, people should only be praised or blamed for using their freedom either well or poorly, i.e. for making good or bad choices. The second component is the feeling of a 'firm and constant resolution' to use one's freedom well such that one can never lack the will to carry out whatever has been judged to be best.

Notice that both components of *générosité* relate to the second and third maxim of the earlier, provisional code. The first component is reminiscent of the third maxim in its acknowledgement of people's freedom of choice and the control they have over their desires. In the provisional moral code, this is a way of avoiding the regret of not achieving some set goal. Here the point is that people can only be praised or blamed for what they will, precisely because only their volitions are in their control. This relates to the third maxim in that a person cannot be blamed for not achieving some goal, since it is beyond his ability and control. But he can be blamed for not changing his desire and the resulting feeling of regret once it is discovered that that goal is beyond his abilities. So, as it turns out, strict adherence to the third maxim of the moral code satisfies the first condition of the later virtue of *générosité*.

The second component relates to the second maxim in that both pertain to firm and resolute action. *Générosité* requires a resolute conviction to use free will correctly, while the second maxim is a resolution to stick to the judgement most likely to lead to a good action unless there is a significant reason for changing course. However, a difference between these two is that the *Discourse*'s second maxim focuses on the correct use and resolute enactment of probable *judgements*, while the later ethics of *générosité* emphasize a firm resolution to use *free will* correctly.[5] But once this decision has been freely made, both systems endorse resolute action in pursuit of the good. This, in turn, should lead to a true state of *générosité* so that people legitimately esteem themselves for having correctly used those faculties, i.e. intellect and will, through which humans are most in the likeness of God.

Descartes further describes the generous person as someone who is in complete command of his passions:

> In particular, they have mastery over their desires, and over jealousy and envy, because everything they think sufficiently valuable to be worth pursuing is such that its acquisition depends solely on themselves; over hatred of other people, because they have esteem

for everyone; over fear, because of the self-assurance which confidence in their own virtue gives them; and finally over anger, because they have little esteem for everything that depends on others . . . (AT XI 448: CSM I 385)

Notice in this passage that a generous person has mastery over herself because of her knowledge that only her choices are truly in her control and are the only real basis for praise or blame. This provides the basis for the esteem she feels for herself and others. Accordingly, the negative feelings of jealousy, envy, fear and anger, which often lead people to commit immoral acts, are absent from the generous person, because she desires and values only those things that are within her abilities. She is in control over anger, because she neither desires nor values things that are not within her control or abilities but depend on others. Nor is she fearful or hateful, because of her esteem for others and the confidence and esteem she feels for herself due to her moral virtue. Descartes concludes section 153 by stating that using one's free will correctly and carrying out what is judged to be best is 'is to pursue virtue in a perfect manner.' Therefore, a person with *générosité* is a moral or virtuous person to the highest possible degree (AT XI 445–6: CSM I 384).

8.6 CONCLUSION

Though it may have seemed strange to group theories of emotions and morals with a discussion of physiology as Descartes did in the *Passions*, it should now be clear as to why this was done. At the core of all this is the theory of the pineal gland as the principal seat of the mind's abilities of perception and will. The passions arise because of certain physiological processes, which cause the pineal gland to move in certain ways in order to move bodily limbs (say to fight or flight) in accordance with other dispositions of body and soul. But the mind's volitions can also cause the pineal gland to move in such a way as to reconstitute those dispositions. For instance, someone predisposed to anger at every slight can develop certain habits that reconstitute that disposition into another such as 'turning the other cheek'. So, free and resolute rational control is essential for mastering the passions, which amounts to a mastering of one's self. This in turn results in the contented, happy and moral life of a truly generous person. So, at the end of his life, Descartes left us with a guidebook for living well, which is the true end of all philosophy.

NOTES

CHAPTER I

1 This example is found in L. J. Beck, *The Method of Descartes: A Study of the Regulae* (Oxford, Clarendon Press, 1952), p. 57. Beck's helpful example is surely based on Descartes's Rule 9 of the *Regulae*, which reads: 'If one tries to look at many objects at one glance, one sees none of them distinctly. Likewise, if one is inclined to attend to many things at the same time in a single act of thought, one does so with a confused mind' (AT X 400–1: CSM I 33).

2 See Principles I.45 at AT VIIIA 21–2: CSM I 205–6.

3 This point is taken from Daniel Flage and Clarence Bonnen, *Descartes and Method: A Search for Method in the Meditations* (London/New York, Routledge, 1999), p. 40–43.

4 This will be discussed in more detail at 2.3 and 2.4.

5 In their discussion of enumeration, Flage and Bonnen focus exclusively on this first function. Although this constitutes only a partial explanation of Descartes' notion of enumeration, they are correct in arguing that enumeration functions in this way in the *Meditations*. Beck, however, recognizes these two functions of enumeration, identifying the second with the 'comprehensive reviews' mentioned in Rule 4 of the *Discourse*. But Beck does not offer a more general, unified account of enumeration as provided later in this section. Instead, Beck maintains that these are two fundamentally different operations with the same name.

6 This point is made in Flage and Bonnen, *Descartes and Method*, p. 43.

7 This argument will be discussed in more detail at 5.6.

8 For a detailed discussion of the connections and differences between Pappus' account of analysis and synthesis and that of Descartes, see Athanassios Raftopoulos, 'Cartesian analysis and synthesis', in *Studies in History and Philosophy of Science*, 34 (2003), 265–308.

9 Here it is important to mention that a full enquiry can begin with an effect, proceed to the discovery of its cause and then proceed backwards from cause to effect. Jean-Baptiste Morin, a noted mathematician of the time, believes that this forms a vicious circle in reasoning. Descartes

responded by pointing out an ambiguity in the term 'demonstrate'. A demonstration from effects to causes constitutes a proof, whereas a demonstration from causes to effects constitutes an explanation (see Letter to Morin, 13 July 1638, AT II 197–8: CSM K 106–7). The point seems to be that a demonstration of cause A from effect B is just a proof that A is in fact the cause of B, but a demonstration of B from A explains or tells the story of how A caused B. It could also be the case that the discovery of cause A can be used to demonstrate or explain another effect C. Hence, analysis shows how first truths were discovered.

10 Although Descartes is the author of the *Meditations*, it is commonly accepted among scholars that its first-person narrator is not Descartes himself but a character developed by him. The evidence for this is that unlike the *Discourse* the *Meditations* are not autobiographical. As a result, this first-person narrator, or 'I', is commonly referred to as merely 'the Meditator' in order to avoid mixing up the character telling the story of his meditation and the author of the work.

11 Descartes himself says basically the same thing at the beginning of Part 4 of the *Discourse* (AT VI 31: CSM I 126–7).

12 A resurgence of interest in ancient Scepticism in the early seventeenth century makes it not all that surprising that Descartes used such scenarios in his own writings but for his own purposes. Some scholars have recently examined Descartes' use of these sceptical scenarios of the Academic and Pyrrhonian schools of Scepticism. This is not the place for making this fascinating comparison. For more on this, see Janet Broughton, *Descartes's Method of Doubt* (Princeton / Oxford, Princeton University Press, 2002), pp. 33–41 and Gail Fine, 'Descartes and Ancient Skepticism: Reheated Cabbage?', in *The Philosophical Review* 109, 2 (2000), 195–234. Yet, even though Descartes denied it, the possible influence of Augustine on Descartes' use of scepticism in finding absolutely certain knowledge, as pointed out by Arnauld in the *Fourth Replies*, is also quite interesting. For more on this, see Stephen Menn, *Descartes and Augustine* (Cambridge, Cambridge University Press, 1998)

13 Janet Broughton convincingly argues for this claim. See Broughton, *Descartes's Method of Doubt*, pp. 64–7.

CHAPTER 2

1 Pyrronhists take their name from the ancient Sceptic, Pyrrho (365–270 BCE), who argued that nothing was certain and, therefore, nothing could be known. Accordingly, Pyrronhists believed that they should not pass judgement on anything whatsoever and merely claimed that things 'seemed' or 'appeared' to be so. As a result, a sincere Pyrronhist would not hold any opinions and since such beliefs are the basis for action, complete inaction is the ideal of the sage. Descartes, however, completely excludes such 'hyperbolic' doubt from the practical domain, limiting it to only his philosophical thinking. Indeed, in Part 3 of the *Discourse*, Descartes lays out a 'provisional moral code' to live by while

engaged in his hyperbolic doubt so as not to be paralysed into inaction. Even though this moral code is not absolutely certain, Descartes is willing to play the odds, so to speak, by arguing that these maxims are more likely than not to guide his conduct in the right direction. This provisional moral code is discussed in more detail at 8.4.

2 This kind of inference from the existence of some thing to the necessary conditions for its existence is known as a transcendental deduction and is commonly associated with Immanuel Kant's deductive method in the *Critique of Pure Reason*. The extent to which Descartes' transcendental arguments are the same or different from Kant's or even more modern conceptions of this type of inference is far beyond the scope of this study, but Broughton discusses it in some detail. See Broughton, *Descartes's Method of Doubt* (Princeton/Oxford, Princeton University Press, 2002), pp. 186–96.

3 'I think, therefore I am' is also the formulation used at *Principles* I.7. See AT VIIIA 7: CSM I 194–5.

4 This manner of reasoning is the reasoning from a property or mode of a thing to the existence of a thing that is the subject in which that property or mode resides. See 3.2 for more on this substance/mode relation.

5 This is discussed in more detail at 5.6.

6 Here it should be noted that at Descartes' time the answer to any 'what' question was supposed to designate the nature or essence of that thing. So, when Descartes asks 'What am I?' he is asking about what it is that constitutes the nature or essence of the 'I' itself.

7 In the *Discourse*, Descartes takes the inference a step further by concluding that the certainty of the mind, or thinking thing that I am, is really distinct from the body, and as such it is possible for the mind to exist without the body. However, he does not come to this conclusion in the corresponding place in the *Second Meditation* but waits until the *Sixth Meditation*. What this real distinction amounts to, the soundness of these arguments, and their implications for the immortality of the soul and union of mind and body into one substantial human being, will be discussed in Chapters 3 and 7, respectively.

8 Descartes makes basically the same distinction in his late work, *Passions of the Soul* (1649). See Part I, sections 17–19 at AT XI 342–3: CSM I 335–6.

9 Of course, these kinds of 'sensory perceptions' are not veridical because they are not caused by actual objects existing outside the mind. Accordingly, they are 'sensations' in the weak sense. Descartes also has much to say about veridical sense perception and how external objects cause them; this discussion will have to wait until Chapter 8.

10 For more on the *Discourse*'s provisional moral code, see 8.4.

11 This leads to the conclusion that animal souls are not immortal, contrary to the views of some at the time, as well as the infamous conclusion that animals do not, strictly speaking, feel hunger, thirst and pain, because a rational soul is required for having these sensations.

CHAPTER 3

1   See Louis Loeb, *From Descartes to Hume: Continental Metaphysics and the Development of Modern Philosophy* (Ithaca, Cornell University Press, 1981), pp. 78–82; and Peter Markie, 'Descartes's concepts of substance', in John Cottingham (ed.), *Reason, Will and Sensation* (Oxford, Clarendon Press, 1994), pp. 63–88. However, some commentators have given up the search for a precise conception of substance in Descartes' philosophy. For this view, see Desmond Clarke, *Descartes's Theory of Mind* (Oxford, Oxford University Press, 2003), pp. 207–34. It is the contention here that Descartes is more precise about his conception of substance than most scholars give him credit for.

2   It is important to note that even though Descartes lists this as a 'definition', it is not for that reason definitive. This account of substance is listed as a definition in a short synthetic, geometrical exposition of the *Meditations*, which was composed in response to a suggestion made at the end of the *Second Objections*. The suggestion was to lay out the definitions, axioms and postulates of his metaphysics and then lay bare the deductions of its main points so that the reader can better follow his arguments. Descartes acquiesces to giving this geometrical exposition of his work but with the caveat that he will not include everything that is included in the *Meditations*. 'And even the items that I do include will not be given a fully precise explanation. This is partly to achieve brevity and partly to prevent anyone supposing that what follows is adequate on its own' (AT VII 159: CSM II 113). Hence, the 'definition' of 'substance' given here should not be taken as definitive because the Geometrical Exposition by itself is not 'fully precise'.

3   It should be noted here that Descartes' use of 'attribute' in this context is not technical. Rather, he is using it in the looser sense of a being that is 'naturally ascribable to something', which also includes modes (see *Comments on a Certain Broadsheet*, AT VIIIB 348–9: CSM I 297).

4   For more on Descartes' doctrine of attributes, see Justin Skirry, *Descartes and the Metaphysics of Human Nature* (London, Continuum, 2005), pp. 53–6.

5   On this account, Descartes would be considered a conceptualist with regard to universals. However, others have interpreted Descartes to be a nominalist in this regard. See Lawrence Nolan's series of articles on this subject: 'Reductionism and nominalism in Descartes's theory of attributes', *Topio*, 16 (1997), 129–40; 'The ontological status of Cartesian natures', *Pacific Philosophical Quarterly*, 78 (1997), 164–94; and 'Descartes' theory of universals', *Philosophical Studies*, 98 (1998), 161–80.

CHAPTER 4

1   Descartes also formulates this argument at *Principles* I.17–18 (AT VIIIA 11–12: CSM I 198–9) and also in the Geometrical Exposition in the *Second Replies* as Proposition II at AT VII 167: CSM II 118.

2   This is not to say that the shape of a dog may not cause someone to

think of a dog. From Descartes' perspective, this would occur when someone already has the idea of a dog and then sees a shape that is reminiscent of the shape that dogs usually possess. Notice that the shape of a dog is not the cause of the existence of the idea of a dog but only that the idea of the shape is associated with an already existing idea.

3   John Locke and David Hume maintain that the idea of God is derived in this way.

4   For more, see Edwin Curley, 'The immortality of the soul in Descartes and Spinoza', *Proceedings of the American Catholic Philosophical Association*, 75 (2001), 27–42.

5   For a more detailed explanation of the traditional account of the Eucharist by Aquinas and Descartes' scholastic near-contemporary, Francisco Suarez, see T. D. Sullivan and Jeremiah Reedy, 'The ontology of the Eucharist', *American Catholic Philosophical Quarterly*, 64 (Summer 1991), 373–86.

6   Here it should be noted that Descartes dilutes his opinion in his response to Arnauld. There he claims that he did not deny the existence of real accidents but only their intelligibility, 'for I firmly insist and believe that many things can be brought about by God which we are incapable of understanding' (AT VII 249: CSM II 173).

7   More will be said about the human body and its relation to the soul in Chapter 7.

CHAPTER 5

1   For a more detailed account of the issues surrounding the doctrines of material and formal falsity, see Deborah J. Brown, *Descartes and the Passionate Mind* (Cambridge, Cambridge University Press, 2006), Chapter 4.

2   Discerning the sense in which the will of a finite thinking thing is 'infinite' is a difficult task that must wait for another time. But for present purposes it is important to recognize that the scope of the will is much greater than that of the intellect.

3   This notion of a 'clear and distinct perception', then, is just a more developed version of the earlier notion of 'intuition' discussed in Chapter 1.

4   Another interesting feature about this is that only those who know that God exists and cannot be a deceiver can have absolutely certain knowledge. Therefore, atheists cannot know anything with absolute certainty.

5   Some commentators maintain that these two versions of the proof of an external world are fundamentally different in that the one found in the *Meditations* somehow relies entirely on natural inclination, whereas the version found in the *Principles* relies explicitly on the doctrine of clear and distinct perception just discussed. See Thomas Vinci, *Cartesian Truth* (New York, Oxford University Press, 1998), and Margaret Wilson, *Descartes* (London, Routledge & Kegan Paul, 1978). However, given the central role of God's non-deceiving nature in both versions, it is evident that they are fundamentally the same despite some superficial

differences. For more on this, see Cecilia Wee, 'Descartes's two proofs of the external world', *Australasian Journal of Philosophy*, 80 (2002), 487–501.

CHAPTER 6

1 For more on Galileo's trial and Descartes' reaction to it, see Desmond Clarke, *Descartes: A Biography* (Cambridge, Cambridge University Press, 2006), Chapter 4.
2 For more on the relation between Descartes' physics as expressed in *The World* and its relation to his physics expressed in the *Principles*, see Daniel Garber, *Descartes's Metaphysical Physics* (Chicago, University of Chicago Press, 1992), especially Chapter 7.
3 This applies not just to inanimate bodies like stones but to any being without a mind, including plants, animals and human automata.
4 Jorge Secada, *Cartesian Metaphysics: The Late Scholastic Origins of Modern Philosophy* (Cambridge, Cambridge University Press, 2000), p. 208. See also Edwin Curley, *Descartes Against the Skeptics* (Cambridge MA, Harvard University Press, 1978), pp. 225–7; and Bernard Williams, *Descartes: The Project of Pure Enquiry* (Sussex, Harvester Press, 1978), pp. 127–9. Although neither Curly nor Williams cite these passages, they would also have to interpret them this way given their other comments on the nature of bodies and space.
5 For more on this, see Denis Des Chene, *Physiologia: Natural Philosophy in Late Aristotelian and Cartesian Thought* (Ithaca, Cornell University Press, 1996), pp. 356–7; and Garber, *Descartes's Metaphysical Physics*, p. 127.
6 For a more in-depth discussion of Descartes' conception of motion and its ramifications for his physics, see Garber, *Descartes's Metaphysical Physics*, pp. 157–72. It should also be noted that Descartes does not settle on the separation of bodies as a useful definition, because this would 'clash too much with our ordinary way of speaking' (AT VIIIA 56: CSM I 235).
7 For more on this, see *Principles* III.46 (AT VIIIA 100: CSM I 256) and see a letter of 30 April 1639 to Debeaune (AT II 543: CSM K 135).
8 Garber, *Descartes's Metaphysical Physics*, pp. 235–7.
9 Here it should be noted that this example and the one in the next paragraph are intended only as ways of illustrating what Descartes means by this third law. They are not fully detailed examples of how this law is supposed to work. Indeed, Descartes tries to give more detailed examples at *Principles* II.46–52. Also for a fuller examination of this law and its application, see Garber, *Descartes's Metaphysical Physics*, pp. 237–42 and 255–62.

CHAPTER 7

1 For a much more thorough logical examination of both real distinction arguments, see Joseph Almog, *What Am I? Descartes and the Mind-Body Problem* (Oxford, Oxford University Press, 2002), especially Chapter 1.

2   Elizabeth is concerned about the possibility of voluntary bodily move-
     ment for moral reasons. For a bodily movement enacting a morally good
     or bad action must be voluntary and not the mere result of mechanism,
     in order for that action and the person performing it to be morally
     praiseworthy or blameworthy.

3   Thomas Aquinas, *Summa Contra Gentiles*, trans. James F. Anderson
     (Notre Dame, University of Notre Dame Press, 1975), p. 169.

4   For a much more thorough account of how the form-matter relation
     works in Descartes, see Paul Hoffman, 'The unity of Descartes's man',
     The Philosophical Review, 95 (1986), 339–69; and Justin Skirry, *Des-
     cartes and the Metaphysics of Human Nature* (London, Continuum,
     2005). However, it should be noted that this is a minority view among
     scholars, and that most understand Descartes' theory of mind-body
     union in ways similar to those of Elizabeth and Gassendi. For a contrary
     view, see Marleen Rozemond, *Descartes's Dualism* (Cambridge MA,
     Harvard University Press, 1998).

CHAPTER 8

1   The principal seat of the soul was a matter of some controversy among
     philosophers at the time. Some followed Aristotle's opinion that it is
     located in the heart, while others thought it was located in the brain. The
     placement of the soul's principal seat in the pineal gland, which is
     located near the centre of the brain, is unique to Descartes.

2   Notice that the workings of human bodies are based on a serious of
     pipes filled with liquids, viz. the circulatory and nervous systems. This
     is a result of the influence of hydromechanics on Descartes' early
     thought. In the *Treatise on Man*, he makes reference to the 'grottoes and
     fountains in the royal gardens' in which 'the mere force with which the
     water is driven as it emerges from its source is sufficient to move various
     machines, and even to make them play certain instruments or utter cer-
     tain words depending on the various arrangement of the pipes through
     which the water is conducted' (AT XI 130–1: CSM I 100). Desmond
     Clarke speculates that Descartes may have even read Salomon de Caus's
     book on the subject. See Desmond Clarke, *Descartes: A Biography*
     (Cambridge, Cambridge University Press, 2006), pp. 92–3.

3   Paul Hoffman argues that sensations and the like are modes that reside
     in two subjects. This is different from the position sketched above where
     a human being is understood to be one, whole subject composed of two
     parts. Hence, on the interpretation offered here, modes of sensation are
     modes of this one, human subject. Unfortunately, this is not the place to
     discuss the pros and cons of these two accounts. But for comparison, see
     Paul Hoffman, 'Cartesian passions and Cartesian dualism', *Pacific
     Philosophical Quarterly*, 71 (1990), 310–33. Also see the discussion of
     'straddling modes' in Deborah J. Brown, *Descartes and the Passionate
     Mind* (Cambridge, Cambridge University Press, 2006), Chapter 5.

4   For more on the final causal or teleological aspects of Descartes' theory
     of sensation, see Alison Simmons, 'Sensible ends: latent teleology in

Descartes' account of sensation', *Journal of the History of Philosophy*, 44 (2001), 49–75.

5   There is more overlap here than might be initially apparent, for a correct use of free will also includes a correct use of judgement since the former is an integral feature of the latter. For more on the role of free will in making judgements, see 5.4 and 5.5.

BIBLIOGRAPHY

Almog, J. (2002), *What Am I? Descartes and the Mind-Body Problem*. Oxford: Oxford University Press.

Aquinas, Thomas (J. F. Anderson, trans., 1975), *Summa Contra Gentiles*. Notre Dame IN: University of Notre Dame Press.

Beck, L. J. (1952), *The Method of Descartes: A Study of the Regulae*. Oxford: Clarendon Press.

Broughton, J. (2002), *Descartes's Method of Doubt*. Princeton/Oxford: Princeton University Press.

Brown, D. J. (2006), *Descartes and the Passionate Mind*. Cambridge: Cambridge University Press.

Clarke, D. (2003), *Descartes's Theory of Mind*. Oxford: Oxford University Press.

—— (2006), *Descartes: A Biography*. Cambridge: Cambridge University Press.

Clatterbaugh, K. (1980), 'Descartes's causal likeness principle', *The Philosophical Review*, 3, 379–402.

Curley, E. (1978), *Descartes Against the Skeptics*. Cambridge MA: Harvard University Press.

—— (2001), 'The immortality of the soul in Descartes and Spinoza', *Proceedings of the American Catholic Philosophical Association*, 75, 27–42.

Descartes, R. (1974–1989, C. Adam and P. Tannery, eds), *Œuvres de Descartes*, 11 vols. Paris: Vrin.

—— (1984–1991, J. Cottingham, R. Stoothoff, D. Murdoch and A. Kenny, trans.), *The Philosophical Writings of Descartes*, 3 vols. Cambridge: Cambridge University Press.

Des Chene, D. (1996), *Physiologia: Natural Philosophy in Late Aristotelian and Cartesian Thought*. Ithaca: Cornell University Press.

Fine, G. (2000), 'Descartes and Ancient Skepticism: Reheated Cabbage?', *The Philosophical Review*, 109, 195–234.

Flage, D., and C. Bonnen (1999), *Descartes and Method: A Search for Method in the Meditations*. London/New York: Routledge.

Garber, D. (1992), *Descartes's Metaphysical Physics*. Chicago: University of Chicago Press.

Hoffman, P. (1986), 'The unity of Descartes's man', *The Philosophical Review*, 95, 339–69.

—— (1990), 'Cartesian passions and Cartesian dualism', *Pacific Philosophical Quarterly*, 71, 310–33.

—— (1999), 'Cartesian composites', *Journal of the History of Philosophy*, 37, 251–70.

—— (2003), 'The passions and freedom of the will', in B. Williston and A. Gombay (eds), *Passion and Virtue in Descartes*. New York: Humanity Books, pp. 261–300.

Kenny, A. (1969), *Descartes: A Study of his Philosophy*. New York: Random House.

Loeb, L. (1981), *From Descartes to Hume: Continental Metaphysics and the Development of Modern Philosophy*. Ithaca: Cornell University Press.

Markie, P. (1994), 'Descartes's concepts of substance', in J. Cottingham (ed.) *Reason, Will and Sensation*. Oxford: Clarendon Press, pp. 63–88.

Marshall, J. (1998), *Descartes's Moral Theory*. Ithaca: Cornell University Press.

Menn, S. (1998), *Descartes and Augustine*. Cambridge: Cambridge University Press.

Morgan, V. (1994), *Foundations of Cartesian Ethics*. New York: Humanities Press.

Murdoch, D. (1993), 'Exclusion and abstraction in Descartes's metaphysics', *The Philosophical Quarterly*, 43, 38–57.

Nolan, L. (1997a), 'Reductionism and nominalism in Descartes's theory of attributes', *Topio*, 16, 129–40.

—— (1997b), 'The ontological status of Cartesian natures', *Pacific Philosophical Quarterly*, 78, 164–94.

—— (1998), 'Descartes' theory of universals', *Philosophical Studies*, 98, 161–80.

Prendergast, T. (1993), 'Descartes: immortality, human bodies and God's absolute freedom', *The Modern Schoolman*, 71, 17–46.

Radner, D. (1971), 'Descartes' notion of the union of mind and body', *Journal of the History of Philosophy*, 9, 159–70.

Raftopoulos, A. (2003), 'Cartesian analysis and synthesis', *Studies in History and Philosophy of Science*, 34, 265–308.

Rozemond, M. (1998), *Descartes's Dualism*. Cambridge MA: Harvard University Press.

Secada, J. (2000), *Cartesian Metaphysics: The Late Scholastic Origins of Modern Philosophy*. Cambridge: Cambridge University Press.

Simmons, A. (2001), 'Sensible ends: latent teleology in Descartes' account of sensation', *Journal of the History of Philosophy*, 39, 49–75.

Skirry, J. (2005), *Descartes and the Metaphysics of Human Nature*. London: Continuum.

Sullivan, T. D., and J. Reedy (1991), 'The ontology of the Eucharist', *American Catholic Philosophical Quarterly*, 64, 373–86.

Verbeek, T. (1992), *Descartes and the Dutch: Early Reactions to Cartesian Philosophy 1637–1650*. Carbondale: Southern Illinois University Press.

Vinci, T. (1998), *Cartesian Truth*. New York: Oxford University Press.

Voss, S. (1994), 'Descartes: the end of anthropology', in J. Cottingham (ed.), *Reason, Will and Sensation*. Oxford: Clarendon Press.

Wee, C. (2002), 'Descartes's two proofs of the external world', *Australasian Journal of Philosophy*, 80, 487–501.

Williams, B. (1978), *Descartes: The Project of Pure Enquiry*. Sussex: Harvester Press.

Williston, B. and A. Gombay (2003, eds), *Passion and Virtue in Descartes*. New York: Humanities Press.

Wilson, M. (1978), *Descartes*. London: Routledge & Kegan Paul.

INDEX